The Exterority Crisis:

from the city limits and beyond

The Exteriority Crisis:

from the city limits and beyond

BERKELEY, CALIFORNIA

The Exteriority Crisis: from the city limits and beyond.

Cover photo by Miguel P. Corrales

ISBN: 978-0-615-25839-3

Additional copies of this book can be ordered from LuLu:
http://www.lulu.com

Oyster Moon Press is a non-profit, surrealist publishing co-op that originated in Berkeley, California.

http://www.oystermoonpress.com

Table of Contents:

Surrealism and exteriority

In its corners, streets, gates, bars, squares, boulevards, gardens, parks and cafés, the city, as is known, maintains some of the focal points of "its" unconscious. These are found and explored everyday by surrealists who obtain the essential experience of surreality in metropolitan life. The concrete experience of exteriority (which in the following collective essay we concentrate only on the city limits and beyond them) requires from us a disposition closely akin not only to the sensible renewal of people (since the greatest promise resides herein), but also to existence and its poetic reserves, and to the revitalization of the interior life that is suffering a process of sterilization because of the convulsive technologization of interiority and the progressive forgetting of life *outside*.

The experience of exteriority begins with a leap past the point where it had been alienated by the metropolitan (culturized) interiorization of the experience, where it became merely delegated and improper. This metropolitan interiorization works as a screen that separates exteriority from its outskirts, which tends to homogenize it, *making it uniform*, diluting its non-duality and its indeterminate nature. To have this metropolitan outskirt restored is thus to overcome an urbanized interiority (cellular, virtual, without community) predetermined by knowledge that is mimetic, clonal, delayed and consequently devitalized, since it doesn't *reveal i*tself (not announcing its place, breaking with its prearranged location) but instead withdraws into a feeble interior, in an advanced stage of sterilility.

In a period when the human spirit (of the individual and of the collective) suffers from great convulsions, pronounced declines and experiences symptoms like the ones that we just described (only a few, although sufficiently alarming), the power with which exteriority can penetrate the human spirit might have the unsuspected value of effecting a renewal on it.

This abandonment to exteriority is not an escape (nor an Edenic return), but the impulse of life towards the reconquest of itself (1), and in the intellectual sphere is one of the most urgent objectives at the beginning of this century. This abandonment is not comparable to the sublimation of the romantic absolute (neither is it a question of comparing it within the frame of this reflection). Perhaps the abandonment to exteriority engenders a somewhat more modest disposition (at least in its first formulation), despite the great depth, as if it were the restoration of the relationship with exteriority through what we could call a lesson from childhood: the discovery within the concrete of the animacy of everything, of *that* which palpitates and which we could associate with an exteriorial unconscious.

By this we think of exteriority as an indeterminate sphere that could contain its own unconscious, or rather, its own animate life, pulsating within concrete objects, spaces and places; and we encounter these items at a limit which this collective essay defines as the one distinguished by the *outskirts* (and what comes thereafter). This is the reason why exteriority can't be confused with nature, or otherwise we would be obliged to include within our interventions for example a reflection on the ecological phenomena in its broadest sense, which is not the case here. Through confining our thought to the outskirts – to those urban spaces on the fringe – we conclude our interventions in a certain way by trying to focus on these specific objects, spaces and places, while deliberately setting aside surrealism's historic interests such as the ones relative to the encounter, objective chance, wandering, unconditional waiting, etc. And by situating this thought beyond the outskirts, we dare *to cross the bridge where the ghosts come to meet us* (2), to find ourselves before everything that lives not according to the predeterminations of history, but which flows with the generative force of original ambiguity.

The following texts and images retrace the development of this growing concern that has emerged in certain parts of the international surrealist movement since the early 1990's, and which represent the concretization of specific investigations.

It is our hope that this book – and especially the reflections and points of view expressed in the most recent writings (3) – not only contributes to the enrichment and actualization of the surrealist experience, but above all will inspire the reader to deepen them in concrete life.

The editors,
Eric W. Bragg, Eugenio Castro, Bruno Jacobs
September 2008

1. And this impulse is about exteriority being defined as a kind of poetic experience, not as a philosophical concept.
2. The sentence comes from the film *Nosferatu: A Symphony of Horror* (1922), by F. W. Murnau.
3. Most of the texts that comprise this book are unpublished, and are accompanied by others that were published before. Refer to the appendix, page 177 for more information.

Worthless Places

by Mattias Forshage

The foremost purposes of city planning are of course purely disciplinary, but it is based on generalised demands for profitability against the world in its areal, material foundation. Most of the land is used, and serves a purpose in one way or another. Everything is demarcated and categorised, built upon, cultivated, worked, or possibly preserved for tourism or recreation with an ideological purpose; it all has its place and its value.

On the other hand, the "non-places" still extant in cities and suburbs gain an ever more important symbolic and poetic meaning: that is, the unused or abandoned interspaces between different planned places. Exceptions remaining or reborn everywhere: hidden corners of parks, odd backstreets and nooks, interspaces between properties, buildings or roads, various pathways and squares left half-ready or abandoned in the quick transformations of urban life. Pedantic city planning creates order much through rejection: an increasing number of places do not fulfill their intended functions. They get demarcated as a vaguely forbidden zone, close upon us but economically dead and therefore often invisible.

The point is of course to prefer the accursed share before all that is enclosed in the service of economical or ideological utility. The worthess in itself. And at the same time the picturesque qualities of these worthless places are often striking. But within the frames of our project concerning worthless places that we've been pursuing for some years in the Surrealist group in Stockholm, we try to go further, and through more systematic study attempt to reveal focuses of resistance where one least expected them.

Many of them are characterised by the fact that odd situations tend to emerge there: one finds strange objects, and becomes witness to – or part of – strange courses of events, that all blossom like mold just because the place isn't pruned, supervised or laboriously restricted to a planned function. Others of these places have no extenuating

qualities, and rather get their value from their total worthlessness.

This systematic effort includes not only photographic documentation, classification and speculation concerning origin and development, but also their study by means of various surrealist inquiries and games (among other things revealing subjective obsessions of these places), collecting anecdotes (stressing their possibilities from a social point of view), and their botanical study, which has turned out to be a key aspect.

Inspired by a book on the flora of Stockholm by botanist Per Sigurd Lindberg we have realised what a unique botanical environment the city (and of course above all its worthless places) really is. It has become such an oasis through a number of particular circumstances; of which most can be described as extremely tough environmental factors; drought, pollution, overnourishment, asphalt, concrete, macadam; the extremely high rate of disturbance (wear as well as total reshaping, through building works, repairs, people, cars); and the profuse exchange with other milieus and other parts of the world (through trade, tourism etc.). All these circumstances contribute in making the city a refuge for involuntarily introduced plants, fugitives from cultivations, various weeds and especially a number of less competitive species that thrive here in the absence of those more competitive species that dominate the natural environments.

Beside the fact that these plants have their own poetry and their particular scientific interest, they may serve as the most concrete aspect of a row of analogous fields.

First the level of meaning: the city gets overgrown wherever the refuse collectors of utility look the other way; what has been abandoned and forgotten gathers in heaps that start to grow in the hidden; a jungle of the strange fruits of the rejected, the revenge of nature or the return of the repressed, a chaos sometimes imaginative and sometimes just disgusting but always strange and profoundly human.

To some extent this is true also concerning the material artifacts, the objects and architecture: the concentrations of garbage, lost belongings, constructions falling apart, solutions having become out of date.

It is definitely true from a social point of view: the homeless, alcoholics, drug addicts, maniacs, curious children, drifting youths, all pay their visits to these non-places to make nonintended use of them and charge them with the excitement of their obsessions. The strange encounters that might result, the strange ways of communication, the strange solutions, in all their nonhandiness ought to be an important element in what really constitutes the social today (not so long ago people used to confuse state with society, but that isn't done as easily today when the state abandons its social or pseudo-social functions one by one).

And contemplating the main tendencies of the development of urban flora: 1) disturbance and overnourishment, 2) indiscriminate internationalisation, 3) the mass immigration and dominance of the less competative, they might prove to be key aspects not only to modern urbanism but to late capitalist society in the entirety of the imperturableness in its disintegration. This would of course include revolutionary possibilities. Never underestimate the worthless.

Ceramics, Tuna-Fisheries and Copper Mines

by Miguel P. Corrales

In the abandoned temples of industrial madness, it is beautiful to witness the triumph of Nature over the calculated forces of the stupid and exploitative intelligence. If the beauty of the old castles and medieval palaces not recuperated by the bourgeois makes us think about the fall of the powerful and of the ruins of industrial archaeology (being worthy of this ludicrous designation), it invites us much better to see the disparity of a world that has always depreciated the essential for the superfluous, the greedy, the glorification of work, the useful and the comfortable as the supreme values - what ideals, what nightmares!

At the same time, these archaeological ruins possess the same "poetic transfer" of which Cirlot spoke, by "the old, corroded, partially destroyed, peeled and cracked walls." It is not without a shudder how this poet, in the same way his great-grandfather, Gustavo Adolfo, is oriented - or disoriented - towards these deserts of catastrophe that are much more preferable than their actual antipodes or the pharaoic commercial centers of the new consumerist planet of garbage.

In Portugal, a country which for the past two decades I have passionately investigated its secular and millennial nature (i.e. preindustrial and pre-eucalyptical), and its moving traditions - a country illuminated by I-don't-know-what, yet already in irreversible extinction and ruined in a certain way also - I have examined three spaces which have brought me that disorientation, that shuddering without which no true impression exists and without which the invisible doors of the unknown could not be opened.

The first of those spaces is actually found scattered among the areas near the central shores of the country. They are the numerous ceramics factories, with their imposing smokestacks and naves, all of them glaring of blood-red bricks. The most spectacular of them could be the one in Pamphilosa, next to the train station where the northern border connects with the Beira Alta. It has not been violated for that long, being recently invaded by a tribe of gypsies, and by contrast of shape, those

immense shadows among hellish furnaces, indecipherable tools, broken windows and stagnant waters, as well as the shouts of the untamed - such natural children of that admirable village. It seems as if the arrival of the gypsies had augmented the *strangeness* of the sensation; it is an old woman completely dressed in black that hangs clothes in a room illuminated by a candle, or the voices that soon appear from a habitation to the side, or the barking that arises from no-one-knows where. Here are some of those spaces which we have been accustomed to calling Kafkian, and that doubtlessly, to the great writer of anarchy and laughter (because this is the way I view Kafka), they would have appeared suitable for a Wellsian scene from *The Process*.

"In us persist the obscure corners, the mysterious landscapes, the blind windows, the dirty patios, the noisy taverns and the hermetic passions. We walk through the wide streets of the new city, but our steps and gazes are indecisive. In our interior we still tremble as in the old streets of poverty. Our heart knows nothing of the works of sanitation. The old, unhealthy city of the Jews we see as no more real than the new, hygienic city that surrounds us."

I find these lines memorable by which Kafka made manifest "the other" that was, to the propagating bourgeois world and their values of functionality and hyper-cleanliness (i.e. the rejection of Life in all of its exuberant, fascinating richness and terror), unsuitable for their cowardice and guilt, unsuitable for the anaesthetized, pasteurized and desiccated bourgeois.

From the Pamphilosa we leave - by train and then boat from Lisbon in order to cross the "Sea of Paja" - to Tavira in El Algarve, in southern Portugal, to the gorgeous mouth of the Gilão river in the region that is called the "four waters." Behind a few pyramids of salt and an almost camouflaged fort against pirates, through roads among flooded grounds and birds in freedom, the low and strikingly lengthy walls of a phantom town await us: Arraial Ferreira Neto (the Superior Blacksmith Encampment), founded in the 1840s by the Algarve Fish Company in order to house the tuna fishermen with their families. Through a worm-eaten doorway, we reach the interior which is divided into two areas: personal dwellings and shops. The entirety displays the air of a small village from the south, with two plazas, five streets and sixty-four Liliputian houses for the more or less four-hundred people who had come to inhabit them. All of it is situated beneath the most beautiful sky of Portugal, and next to the ocean and a river. The entrance building, a round, fortified tower where the Company's offices are situated, exhibits above the old, golden wall some pleasant and colorfully glazed ceramic tiles, of four fish in the sea - a unique indulgence, together with the small naïf tiles of the school, found in the middle of such disaster. Three of the streets also have their names volutedly inscribed on these tiles (this quite popular Portuguese art): in this manner, the street of Patrón João Lopes (1800-1890), a "meritorious Algarvian seafarer" and the originator of the Company in 1835, with his name among two anchors and a harpoon. Everyone remembers the savage art of catching tuna - almost mythical, as that of the whale hunt in Madeira and above all, in the Azores Islands.

The overturned safe, found in the middle of the Company's main hall within the fortified tower, among a multitude of forever useless papers, makes the most symbolic statement to us. In the tavern from where I carry away a curious checkbook of sales to ships from the 50s (whose bills should have been signed "master of the ship") the marble counter and the wooden crossbeams sigh for the abolition of contradictions, or from the burning waters - although not exclusively - that would come from the hours of suffering and poverty. Through here, after the dismantling of the Company, some years passed and there wandered beneath the de Chirican arches some refugees of the colonial wars, who finished destroying what remained, although for an unknown purpose. These silent, lonely and ghostly places now only serve the wanderings of the mind.

What attracts us more than the stripped houses of the fishermen are the innumerable shops, all replete with memories of tuna fishing. In one, nets and poles are accumulated; another surprises us with an unknown dialogue between two watchtowers; the next one chaotically stacks tens of enormous barrels; in one to the side, a rope creates the most enigmatic figure; in another, worthless boats and oars; another still, with a hundred baskets; far away, where a stupid cot presides, a door on the floor receives us as if below it would lead somewhere; and here, finally, three broken chairs of dark wood represent a horrific judgement (as all judgements are, ultimately), with two of them interrogating a definitively subdued third one.

With all of this, nothing can be compared to the apotheosis of the desolation that awaits us in the São Domingos Mine, a few kilometers from Guadiana and the border of Huelva, where the Baixo Alentejo ends to give way to Algarve. To speak here of "rare beauty," as a magnetic needle would point, is almost euphemistic. Ghostly beauty, atrocious, pitiless and underneath a violent light on eroded soils that would all be a challenge to the most hallucinatory of colorist painters - to a multiplied Tamayo, for example; and what extraordinary textures, as of rough lunar soils, those of fragments of divided and anguished grounds. The São Domingos Mine is the most terrible space of all Portugal.

Exploited since the time of the Romans, in 1858 the Portuguese became modern, through an English concessionary of the Spanish company La Sabina, and until its definitive close in 1966. More than a hundred years of the exploitation of land and men explain the breadth of all that is found here. The town, unchanged since 1966, is the most impeccable example of traditional alentejano architecture bearing the stamp of honest labor, practically without any of the adulterations which the last decades have foisted upon the entirety of the country; a true paradise of plasticity and fairness, in the Moorish reign of tile and cement with the characteristic hermeticism of the popular, architectural creations of Portugal. It was only until a few years ago that the magisterial water-man went from door to door with his cart (painted with the typically vibrant colors of the south), a couple of mules, and a blue, wooden drum. Beautiful carts are remarkable here and there, in fact, as are the horses, ducks, burros, little pigs and ultimately the entire rural world, that complemented the life of the miner. Upon the departure for Serpa, a doll-like house beckons us, next to a statuette of a woman with a pitcher, with the taste for edification in the old-fashioned and extremely Portuguese style: "good day, good voyage." Perhaps it is the only thing that remains of the "happy and pleasant aspect" of which a chronicler spoke in the 50s, when the Mine had more than three-thousand inhabitants (those days there were some seven hundred that chose not to leave). Yet the remnants of the theater, hospital, library or post office no longer remain (or are unrecognizable), even though they are survived by the market (of 1951), the football field (the "Cross Brown Playing Field," 1952) and the movie house, with its green screen for the "program," although in front. The tennis court, beside the remnants of the music kiosk, and surrounded by iron benches equally victimized by the invisible bombardment of time, is reduced to a skeleton, requiring us to make it out with difficulty, so that we remember the reflection of Bernardo Soares: "The beauty of the ruins? It still serves nothing." All of it, in a very broad space which was maintained in the shade by an abundance of trees, and which in its corners the "palace" of the English is displayed, was once visited by the ridiculous queen of England; of course to its side we have the soldiers' barracks of the Republican National Guard, always quick to defend the capitalists and beat down the miners. In 1929, at the request of the miners, the Mine was visited by the celebrated novelist Ferreira de Castro, who wrote in the periodical *O Século* a rapidly censured report that would only become published after the dissolution of the dictatorship as well as the mine itself. The "Central Barber's shop" of Francisco Pires Guerreiro, with its atmosphere of the 1940s or 50s, conjointly exhibits erotic photographs and communist declarations. Another Guerreiro, an old miner, displays his amazing paintings of the Mine in its golden years among the walls of the various bars. Because of the memories that reside in the Mine, the humiliation and slavery coexist with the nostalgia of a time in which life was present, where everyone was young and there were celebrations, dances and castigas - and I do not know of popular poetry more intensely keen and lyrical (and obsessively romantic) than that of the Portuguese village.

In this manner, as if uprooted from a chapter of *Pedro Páramo,* and upon daybreak, en route to Guadiana, I remember a dialogue with an old miner who did not hide his pride for the splendid Mine of yesteryear, despite the signs of the silicosis or respiratory disease which constantly interrupted his words. For her part, the sweet and cordial señora María Joana Gonçalves, in her small, green food store (also very 50's-ish) at the town entrance, has retained from the past the weights, the coffee grinder, the codfish knife, the board of thread spools, which speaks of the suffered life as much as the solidarity and joy of people.

All of this constitutes the "friendly" side of the Mine. There is nothing tragic if we limit ourselves to renting a room in the only guesthouse, as do the sport-fishermen who come to the nearby dam, and to strolling through the old village (but less so if it is August), in which everything is fleetingly animated by the return of those

who mainly work in the industrial area that faces Lisbon. Here is definitely a different atmosphere from any other town of Alentejo. We take a few more steps and find ourselves in front of the four or five cypresses of a small, abandoned cemetery; with some difficulty, the history of young Englishmen can be read on the tombstones, whether killed at sea, by tuberculosis or on course to the Mine. And if we penetrate through to a neighboring road, we find a physically brutal and wrenching drop which is impossible to ignore; there is a gigantic void where "strong waters" lie immobile in its abysmal depths. The walls of this stagnant lagoon possess the shape of a ziggurat, with each step more than three meters in length, creating a succession of intense colors. By circling the opening with caution inspired by the stories of more than one person who had already fallen in, it actually looks like a rickety armchair, and far away, like the skeleton of a sheep.

Starting from here begins the excavated valley made for the extraction of mineral products: ruins everywhere, and nature recovering its rights and re-emerging on all sides. Pulley wheels, wagons, rusted chains, corroded remains of girders, iron bridges and well towers...A little further ahead, we see the station of the train line that transferred the copper pyrites to the port of Pomarão on the Guadiana river, eighteen kilometers below. Only the walls remain, with some sufficiently disturbing graffiti, and the roof - more like giant yellow spools of cables and another artifact with an unknown purpose, which looks like a small iron pan or a ship anchored to the bottom. The valley narrows over the next two kilometers, along which we advance among canals of dark waters, along the path of the train, whose rails were removed decades ago. The smell of the nearby eucalyptus, that was planted in order to retain the soil, is quenched by the ferocious intensity that emanates from these low places and that catches the wind. In the surrounding hills are the ruins of small villages, the only ones that remained standing - such sad sentinels, those leprous walls. Above the enormous, decapitated smokestack of the smelting furnaces there suddenly appears the nest of a stork which cannot counteract the bad augury of a flock of crows that start to cackle and swoop during the rare times that anyone dares to venture close to these places. The valley finally widens to give way to the most oneiric and overwhelming space of the entire route; it might be said that we are within a volcanic landscape of unlimited color. Here, the towers of ceramic tile factories seem to be at the point of crumbling away, and perhaps only a shout is needed to make this happen. Face to face, with ominously open eyes, they maintain a monstrous dialogue - or perhaps they defy each other, so ridiculously high above?

Mounds of debris remain here and there on the eroded ground. In this rarified scene, on a midday of July, 1994, I stood perplexed before the apparition of a red ball of string, tied to a stone resting on top of a wall; nothing less predictable, nothing more enigmatic...

The route to Pomarão, although practical when following the path of the derailed tracks, is hardly recommended, with no less than twenty-nine viaducts and seven tunnels - some flooded and full of brambles - and in the efforts to avoid these, we would probably soon find ourselves lost. The arrival in Pomarão is dazzling, with the village situated within an amphitheater next to the Guadiana and the ruins of the dock where the minerals arrived to be loaded onto six ships. Like the Mine, Pomarão now lives only in memories. And almost the same could be said of the surrounding towns: Salqueriros, Bens, Santana de Cambas, Sapos...or the admirable Montes Juntos, just two kilometers along the battered road from the Mine, between the train line and the Chança river, the natural border with Spain.

A ribeira quando anch
vai de pedrinha em pedrinha
O homem que leva a barca
leva meu bem na barquinha

I went there, in Montes Juntos, where I heard, during an unforgettable nightfall beneath the moon of July, this beautiful alentejano song uttered by a sad and rousing voice that suddenly invaded the silent night. The voice of poetry, eternal alchemy, the only treasure we have, scratched the torrid night during the demise of the Mine of the Red Ball - abandoned thirty, a hundred, or thousands of years ago.

The water is rising on the shore
it goes from stone to stone
the man who leads the skiff
takes my love away in the little skiff

The Sound of Chains: The Gothic Sentiment within Industrial Archaeology

by José Manuel Rojo

"If it can be imagined, then it can be made." This sentence, exultant and brilliant like an oracle or watchword, does not really celebrate the triumph of the imagination, but instead its overwhelming defeat: it is the slogan of a well-known TV commercial that confuses the imagined desire with an object of consumption. Another recent advertisement insisted on asking what is the limit of our desire ("Can't you imagine something better?") to find it incarnated in the form of... an automobile. What surprises us here is not so much the manipulation of the imagination and of desire, but the reaffirmation of the promises of advertising and the world of the consumer as the only imaginary things possible. No longer can anyone doubt that *the television screen shows us only the socially-acceptable formulations of all desires* (1). It is feared that aside from these artificially induced desires, no longer can any other desires be felt; that far away from what we are imagining, the Imaginary does not survive. If it is certain that a point exists where all human behavior remains processed and caught within the inertia of the system, we will accept that this limited area is found external to the realm of the imagination, perhaps even occupying its place. It follows that this system requires a mental classification that would facilitate the physical classification of human desires (even the most obscure and secret desires) so that they could be translated into objects and (super)experiences of consumption. In this manner a wild hunt of the imaginary has been organized, a *project of liquidation* that, according to Annie LeBrun, *consists of assigning a name, an origin, a place, a form, and comprehensively, an identity to anything that doesn't already have one. This involves paying attention to shifting thoughts, organizing fantastic travels, and detaining the flight of dreams. Practically, there is no fantasy today that doesn't have its shape, its weight, and correlatively, its price* (2). Any operation that allows the degradation of desire in the commodity and the systematic control of whatever spirit of revolt will, when isolated from the inspiring soils of the imagination, wither and limit itself to pondering the old, revolutionary ideologies, or even worse, collide with Realism.

Not intending to act upon the outside world, accepting everything as it is, allowing itself to be converted into what it is through hypocracy, through opportunism, through cowardice, disguising itself with the colors of the environment — that is realism. It appears that today this definition of René Crevel's still pervades not only the political situation, but also the entirety of human existence. Will you dream today? Will importance be given to dreams, to the oneiric processes, to the interrogation of those diurnal fantasies behind which are hidden our most terrible, and as such, most necessary desires? I don't think so, or very little, and the results are apparent. The weakness of the forces opposed to the system, despite this or that victory or hopeful note, is attributed to that realism which, consciously or not, we have accepted as a vital norm and which by default negates utopian thought.

It's there that we witness a certain *drop in tension* in the projects of liberating the human being, that become concentrated in a necessary and robust fight *against* neoliberalism, fascism, racism, patriarchy... yet perhaps forgetting that *real life* toward which they are doubtlessly headed anyway (3). I'm not ignoring the fact that, many times, in the daily struggles, new ways of life are improvised far removed from theoretical speculation. If only the defeat of the enemy could be really anticipated, guaranteeing by itself only the triumph of freedom. Maybe also this concept of freedom is too weak when supposing it already made — intact, shining and perfect — waiting only for the end of its captivity, always equal to itself in whatever moment in history, preparing for nothing more than for it to be lived and enjoyed. All would then consist of defending and reclaiming freedom. But as was already said in a surrealist declaration from 1966, *today freedom needs less defenders and more inventors.* It has nothing to do with reclaiming anything. We are not necromancers intending to raise the dead. The force of freedom exists by continuing to be *the great unknown*: our weakness is not knowing how to recognize it, enclosing it in worn-out definitions, preventing us from conceiving it with a new body, with a thousand bodies. This erotization of freedom undoubtedly outweighs the satisfaction of material necessities, goodness and happiness, and it identifies with Jim Mahoney when, durng the reign of abundance in the city of Mahagonny, he protests because *something is missing even though nothing has happened,* and this impassive state becomes intolerable.

Even though nothing has happened. This excessive affirmation, almost nihilistic, this desperate faith in the impossible and in the search at all costs for the philosopher's stone of miracles, this definitive breakdown of conformism forever exposes the false promises of the economy ("Have you seen what is happening," mocks another recent advertisement. Nothing, nothing, NOTHING), and it raises the discussion of freedom to its highest level, from which it still cannot lower itself, retreat from, or adulterate. So what must happen for freedom to realize itself? Simultaneously, everything that the imagination contemplates and decides, with its most original desires, and the unique capacity to provoke *the most wholesome doubts on the great concept of "rational" freedom as it is understood in a society founded on inequality* (Breton). I insist in not speaking of "reclaiming desire," because for these desires the moment of inventing them has arrived (we completely destroy all *fetishism of the reclamation*, a new mechanism of separation that only moves people away from the objects that they wish to reclaim). We are then located in the only possible plane, which consists of the urgent need to formulate an idea of freedom that shatters the "freedom" that the system offers to the ruling class: to formulate and to name, not to defend or reclaim.

But the invention of freedom and desires undergoes a necessary and unavoidable reactivation of the imagination — a phenomenon more complicated and difficult than that which inspires general self-complacency and the mundane. Now if *the imaginary is the space of desire*, there are also imaginary spaces where the same imagination dresses its wounds and is reborn, real spaces that a poetic force attracts and repels at the same time from the real and from the fantastic, *neither objective nor subjective* spaces, *obsolete* spaces capable of provoking unusual thoughts in the human — glimmers of the marvelous, profane illuminations, bold decisions. Spaces and places like *observatories of the interior sky...observatories already in existence naturally in the outside world* (4).

Spaces like the *castle.*

Since the eighteenth century, when it appeared as an indis-

-pensable stage and fundamental protagonist in the gothic novels of Walpole and Maturin, the castle will be a privileged center of modern sensibility, in which the most adventurous forces will take hold. Thus, in the castle, bourgeois reason will shakingly collide with its hidden double — anger and disrespect — which was thought forever exiled and which will undoubtedly nourish the most exacerbated Romanticism. And from the castle of Otranto to the castle of Axel, from the castle of Dracula to the Castle of Eduardo Manostijeras, from the castle of Melisenda to the castle of Argol, it is the castle — or actually within its *ruins* where often men and women have more easily achieved the materialization of their ghosts.

However, the life of a symbol or myth is not eternal: time weathers them, as much as its weathers the stones from the ruins. It would then be said that the poetic spirit perhaps experiences a certain routine and strain when wandering through the castle's secret corridors. Already the enchantments are not as effective, and the dreams, marvels and omens resemble the rigid formulas of a scholasticism of the imagination, anticipated by others with its rules and traps, predictable and sterile as an amusement park, or any social game. *The deepest emotion of existence*, that which is born in *the vicinity of the marvelous, in that point at which human reason loses its control* (Breton), begins to find itself uncomfortable in the imaginary space of the castle.

Perhaps because of this reason, Gilles Ivain affirms that *we know that a modern house could be built which would not necessarily resemble a medieval castle, but which would retain and multiply the poetic power of the castle (Formulation for a new urbanism, 1953)*. And in an anonymous text, *La Frontière Situationiste* (I.S., no. 5, 1960), the situationists propose the *detournement* of buildings and other architectural forms that for a long time popular sensibility has recognized as *affective elements of the environment*, citing as an example the *castle*. And what if that other type of construction were returned (distorted) in such a way that it inherited or better reincarnated the *affective atmosphere* of the castle, extending its legacy to new meanings, to other deliriums?

Precisely, in the text already cited, *Limits not Frontiers*, André Breton asks if there is a fantastic place at that moment (1937) which could replace the castle as a point of attachment for the human psyche, concluding that *everything leads us to believe there is no question of it being a factory*. What is interesting here is not so much the negative conclusion but the consideration of the idea itself — the hypothesis of the factory as a new and imaginary space. Undoubtedly then, the factory of the 1930's (that still maintained a cycle of splendid productivity) *was unable to surpass* the castle, but today we find ourselves at the threshold of new sensible forces that draw our attention to a transcendental change of direction in the realm of the human imagination.

Because this change is now occurring, it has already generated a *gothic sentiment within the archaeology of industry* that transforms the factory, in its abandoned ruins, into a new, imaginary space.

Whoever passes through the splendid desolation of a factory or industrial site in disuse will surely recognize its exultant and poetic power, as the conclave of its mysteries. They are *places that invite one to dream* (5). But in order to get to this state, both the factory and (in its day) the castle had to suffer a decadence that, paradoxically, ended up liberating these places from themselves. The castle and the factory, symbolic and material centers of feudal or bourgeois power, both organized and controlled the social, economic and political life within the area that they occupied. What should one think, for instance, of the complex mine of Hornu found in the surroundings of Mons, that in the 1820's relied on four hundred houses, offices and outbuildings, and where resided 2500 people? How can this not be compared with those medieval fortresses that created around themselves first a hamlet and then a city?

But the castle was vacated and demolished with the advent of capitalism and industrialization, and from its scandalous obsolescence and lack of practical meaning it ceased to represent a threat to freedom and instead became a favorite place for fantasy, myth, as well as extravagance. Today the factory experiences an analogous process, being abandoned by the power of the third sector and the sham economics that for the most part sacrifice a good part of labor to the new and cruel mutation of the system, as was done to the peasants who once migrated to the city in search of work.

And in the outskirts of cities, incongruently embedded in their historical centers, the empty factories wait for us, beckoning to us with siren songs that call for *dreaming*, not odious work.

Nevertheless, what does this magic of the old factories consist of, which I have spoken of so much, perhaps so gratuitously? For a start, of its dismal abandonment, of its manifested uselessness. Far away from whatever practical dangers, outside of the original context that asphyxiated it, the factory ruin is open to self-discovery and is available to everyone. It is necessary to definitively reject all cultural forces that aspire to convert industrial archaeology into a style — protected and restored, processed and packaged in the museum or official institution — ultimately normalized to become precipitated in a historicist reification as that which was enacted by Viollet-le-Duc, which in the opinion of Annie LeBrun, *does not search for but only erases, negates and forgets the frightful lyrical improvisations of the time, with the sole purpose of restoring the document to its reality or to its semblance of functional and architectural reality*. Would this possibly have anything to do with breaking away from the *revolutionary energies* which, according to Walter Benjamin, possess the *antiquated* and which perceive *the first factories*, within the first constructions of iron, among other objects? Does the affective force of the abandoned factory exclusively reside in feeding that revolutionary energy, which Michael Löwy interprets as *a sign of precariousness, of hisoricity, of the mortality of structures, monuments and institutions of the bourgeois?*(6) Or in the exalted memory of the proletarian struggles that convulsed the factories and which today still permeate those places with the contagious vibration of unquenched rebellion and unfulfilled desire? The issue of industrial archaeology certainly occurs here, but not exclusively.

The factory is ultimately a self-imposed imaginary space, by way of the strangeness and mystery that its empty spaces inspire (of which most of us don't know its exact function) and of the ominous grandeur of its own architecture and dimensions. Like the Greeks who believed Micenean architecture to be the work of the cyclops and not of man, we still do not know by whom and for what purpose these disdainful factories were constructed. You leave them feeling excessively high or very low; channels or furrows that cross a habitation; anxious reservoirs. In the Pacisa factory in Madrid, for example, the balcony of one pavilion had the extraordinary shape of the *keel of a ship*. What could be dreamed there when sleeping — closed night — but that which has already been forever *adrift*?

A second factor of surprise is the discovery of extravagant objects — remnants of machinery or useless tools — whose practical

function eludes us in all cases and which defy the mechanisms of strictly rational interpretation, opening them to the lyrics of the improbable and inaugurating a titanic bestiary of extraterrestrial fossils, corroded metal and cables in hibernation. There are also other objects, deposited by chance over time — objects desensitized and silenced through daily use — that in the magic trademark of the factory (itself the *found object*), undergo combustion and illuminate the mental night. It is thus like a simple *red ball, attached to a pebble placed on top of a wall*, appearing in the *rarified scene* of a Portuguese copper mine abandoned since the 1960's which can transform into the key to our destiny: *nothing less predictable, nothing more enigmatic* (7).

Other times, the invasion of the elements consumes the factory as a result of the latter's industrial aggressiveness, moreover creating irrational landscapes that are far removed from reality. In this manner the textile factory of Manresa became bloodied, inundated by the flooding of a river that left behind a layer of red clay tattooed with cracks like scars, a cracked and perturbing floor. There are also contaminating aggressions or industrial pollutions that doubtlessly create (how involuntarily clear) the sacred atmosphere of fairy tales: near Bilbao, an indigo factory in disuse *has managed to stain the surrounding area blue*, evoking the azure of Mallarmé.

And what can be said of the Asland Cement works of Poble de Lillet (Barcelona)(8) which is situated a thousand meters high, straddling the mountain — partially destroyed, decrepit and caught in an unstable equilibrium with the rock — perhaps waiting for the shout of love or rage that would finally shatter the witchcraft that still sustains it, sending it into the abyss that it secretly longs for...The Asland Cement works is the ruins of the castle, it is *the home of ghosts.*

It has already been said that the abandoned factory as an imaginary space is, in the clever expression of Annie LeBrun, *neither objective nor subjective*; a definition that doubtlessly does not situate it under the puerile reign of fantasy without consequences. Sometimes, by chance, the unconscious desire is reconciled with real events, occurring such that the limits of the imagination undergo social convulsions.

In this manner the imaginary space recreates itself in alternative space. If it is true that *the youth movement* of popular culture *(...) Is the first to display a loyalty to the social struggle that requires its own time and place* and also to *the elaboration and construction of situations that find in homeless dwellings the enchanted miniature that aspires to enchant the world* (9), we shouldn't be surprised that, in an unconscious manner, the ghosts, desires and imaginary stimuli that infest the abandoned factories have infiltrated the *active culture* of new revolutionary movements, fertilizing them and inspiring new affective states, new passions, new behaviors and thus new social relations.

"House of the homeless, house of enchantment." This homeless watchword emphasizes the pleasure that a condemned house — destined for inspection or demolition — can *feel* in homeless lyricism, returning it to a new and free existence. But wouldn't it also mean that the squatter's house simultaneously remains *enchanted* in the magical sense — i.e. bewitched, infused with the marvelous, and converted into a distorted space that summons the ghosts or fantasies of the subversive imagination?

We remember that, through mere practical reasons (available space, legal abandonment, administrative neglect...), the empty factories have been occupied by homeless people frequently. I will not dispute the fact that those places which are endowed with so many possibilities can also be uncomfortable and dangerous, and that the collectives that occupy them are committed, at least in the beginning, to the resolution of urgent problems and to their self-defense against the "law," perhaps allowing little time and energy for the poetic dream. But once again: just this? Do they possibly seem oblivious to the amazing seductions of the imaginary space which they now inhabit? In light of the pragmatic and *present-day* demands of the daily struggle, the *obsolescence* of the factory's gothic feeling becomes apparent. The result will not be the exclusion of either dream or action, and not their quick, illusory reconciliation, but instead the resulting exasperation of these two phenomena when they will leave mutually fortified: only the dominant realism will remain as evidence, and in an *injured* form.

There is then a trail of gunpowder, a conductor of heat, a transmitting wire between the imaginary space and the space of the daily struggle that allows the flow of poetic energy between the two, spreading itself and amplifying the spirit of subversion. I'm not only referring to the proliferation of graffiti, on the walls of houses occupied by the homeless, which surpasses its simple aggressiveness by frequently pronouncing the transforming language of poetry (which in itself is a lot); I also consider that instance where the word REVOLT was written on the smokestack (last relic of a vanished factory) that rose within the Ronda de Toledo, next to the Plaza del Campillo Nuevo (Madrid) — on that *smokestack* and not on any other structure: here we see intersected, with visions of fire, practical sense in search of a substrate with adequate height for the visual impact desired, and poetic sense that becomes exalted in the irrational attraction of the smokestack, first symbol of industrial archaeology, distant sister of the castle tower, descendent of the ziggurat, and, last but not least, an inheritor of legendary fame.

This insurgent convulsion sometimes consumes buildings very far removed from the factory. Thus it appears that a certain gothic brilliance infiltrated a neighboring house used by the homeless on 15 Lavapies Street (Madrid) when, during a police eviction (8/10/1996), the resisting homeless occupants disguised themselves as unassailable *ghosts*, covering their faces with white masks and disappearing over rooftops while the police painstakingly searched an abandoned house. (This is nothing less than a magnificent example of *poetry in action.*)

Would these tactics gestate within the shelter of the beating walls of a factory occupied by the homeless, or perhaps before, by some of the building's creators who had once resided there? At the point where the rebellious products of the insatiable imagination begin to materialize, crushing the objective data, the facts of order and statistical realities? Has the *invention of freedom* just been suggested then? It is still too soon for an answer. But here and there the smoke signals warn us of the unavoidable fires that will reanimate the factories. Between their passionate calls we become happily excited, like intoxicated witches in an ecstatic dance: it has arrived — as of yet, this is one helluva party.

---

1. Luis Navarro, *Fogonazos*, *Salamandra* #8/9, 1997-98, p. 5.
2. Annie Le Brun, *Les châteaux de la subversion*, Pauvert, 1982, p. 22.
3. *I ask myself if, finally, we haven't been led astray, if this strike had not really been a hoax... There was the need for a social ideal, which we didn't have.* This insight was expressed by a railway worker who participated in the French strikes of December, 1995 [cited by *Encyclopédie des Nuisances* in *Observaciones sobre la paralysis de Deciembre de 1995*, Virus, 1997, p. 13.
4. André Breton, *Limits not frontiers of surrealism*, in *What is Surrealism: selected writings*. Edited and introduced by Franklin Rosemont, Pathfinder Press, 1978, p. 199.
5. Enrie Kagots, *U.T.O.P.I.A.*, rev. *Ekintza zuzena* #21, 1997, p. 60.
6. Michael Löwy, *Walter Benjamin and surrealism*, *Salamandra* #8/9, p. 10.

7. Miguel P. Corrales, *Ceramics, tuna-fisheries, and copper mines, Salamandra* #8/9, p. 77.
8. Thanks to Lola Marin for the conversations about this cement factory and the Panos de Manresa Factory.
9. Karen Eliot, *Okupacion Global*, rev. *Amano*, #6.

The Presence of Emptiness

by Bruno Jacobs

The poetic experience is more the result of a disclosure, of a revelation than of some inspiration that rather is a consequence of it.

The search for images rich of potential that not only escape but perhaps are even able to counteract the inflation of one-dimentional images that we are subject to today (whether they be the product of the spectacle or of "art," which to a large extent has become its more esoteric part) finds support in the heritage from childhood, namely its spontaneous even if diffuse "metaphysics." The curious look of the child precedes thought and learning, the "cultural heritage" and its aesthetical and ideological implications – how unconscious or indigent, how elaborate or subtle they may be. This leads us out to reality, to places in the tangible world where restless movement ceases and the noise silences, where "material imagination" and meditation are being granted room and can reclaim their right, where confidential experience gets the opportunity to ferment and germinate.

"Metaphysics"

Childhood's metaphysical sense…

In connection with this, the earlier works from the 1910s of painter Giorgio De Chirico appear naturally as an interesting reference: "There is a strange and profound poetry, infinitely mysterious and solitary, which has its basis in the *Stimnung* of an autumnal afternoon when the weather is clear and a low sun casts a longer shadow than in the summer months. It is the extraordinary sensation that you experience in Italian cities and in some of the cities of the Mediterranean coast (…)" (1).

But for De Chirico, it really wasn't even a question of painting "metaphysically," but rather to catch an "other," metaphysical dimension of the world that would exist beyond us. De Chirico rather aesthetisized and manipulated reality because of certain ideas, transcendental preoccupations and a kind of mediumistic vision: an *artist.* If he was inspired by childhood experiences, Shopenhauer and Nietzsche inspired him at least as much.

This "metaphysical" ambience seems to build on a latent or diffuse tension that imbues the physical presence of certain for the most part insignificant places strengthened by stillness, relative silence and a certain desolateness. Also the prevailing light used to be of decisive importance, as if the air started to become visible and time became manifest in a peculiar, physical way, as if the constituitive details were radiating, as if we could behold the time that has elapsed since their origin.

These are places where stillness gets a disquieting effect – *the full presence of emptiness.*

It is actually the casual and unusual that all of a sudden feel more real, and often also the absence of human presence (or rather, the traces of human presence) that create a condensation in time that is poetic to its nature.

Urban environments, certain roofs, façade cornices, certain shrubs especially in sunny and hot summer afternoons or nights for that matter; a stillness that sometimes is accentuated by isolated breezes.

And maybe above all certain industrial environments and ruins about which Miguel P. Corrales so simply and appropriately could write that: "Now these silent, ghostly solitudes only serve the wandering of the mind," and whose significance José Manuel Rojo has illustrated (2).

Possibly also a northern counterpart: deserted areas such as desolate mountain areas, parts of the North American West, northern Scandinavia or Siberia where the loneliness, mystery and majesty of nature is being emphasised particularly during motionless bright summer nights (3). And what about the pictures from the surface of Mars, a world that until quite recently had never been seen because of its inaccessibility and virginity, and which are precisely so strong – much more so than the pictures from the Moon for example – because they are not particularly surprising?

But maybe these latter environments relate more to only one element that is being amplified, namely the loneliness of things.

We come to a standstill, dissolve into the surroundings, and life seems to stop.

The enigmatic in certain places at certain moments – that

special calm as well as the more or less disturbing ambience – is of course not "mystical" at all and doesn't need to be mystified either. But neither does it catch our attention without reason, as if we happened to behold a kind of concretised and fascinating mirror image of some of our mind's tendencies in it, maybe what Freud considered as an inherent tendency to move from the tensions of life back to an inorganic state (4). The immediate, physical and straightforward poetry of such places is probably one of the strongest expressions for what could be termed a charged poetry of stillness in contrast with a dynamic poetry of movement in which other tendencies prevail, but which nonetheless would correspond to fundamental features of the mind.

Perhaps the urge to interpret or aesthetize such places is then a reaction against, a sublimation of that latent terror that they would be able to cause.

"Materialist"

Thus it is a question of a kind of materialist "metaphysics." It is precisely the objective character of such places under these conditions that triggers the subjective experience, and nothing else. Today it is moreover justified in turning away from the irritating "cult of the ego," from prioritising more or less arbitrary personal interpretations and/or misplaced impositions with aspects that do not exist there, or downright mystifying or spiritualising it with what could implicate philosophically (even if that latter kind of activity also has contributed in fruitful or hilarious ways). Rather than use or even reproduce places in order to create certain, often aesthetical effects – like De Chirico and many symbolists and later Paul Delvaux or Edward Hopper – it is appropriate to emphasise the step toward concrete experience (5).

Our eyes are certainly not neutral, and we will always be guilty of certain projections – there also resides a tension or contradiction. But why not ponder emptiness? To *rouse* – like surrealist Paul Nougé aimed at – isn't it in the nature of poetry to confront the world and the conditions of life in a most direct and immediate way as possible?

Prints

But even reproductions – above all, photographs – succeed sometimes in representing and even accentuating the totality, the stillness and the silence that characterise these places, or perhaps mostly in "saving" those elements from time, in "immortalising" them and thereby preserving and even strengthening their metaphysical character (old photographs of certain urban environments with only a few people present for example).

Isn't the "essence" of photography – these ghosts and light captured by chemicals – metaphysical or "concretely metaphysical"? Photography is by no means as objective as one readily wants to think, but can, because of its "documentary" character, be used in a different way than painting, or even language for that matter, with its deceitfulness and arbitrariness.

An old stereotypical example of all this remains the countless, unwearied sunset photographs. For sure it deals with a more dramatic, too general, very conventional and particularly worn out type of "materialist metaphysics," but is however an interesting case as it is, despite everything, precisely because of the combination of calmness and uneasiness and the particular actualisation of time that characterises these sunsets and make them synonymous with poetry in the eyes of the broad public.

Is popular opinion lying?

---

1. *Memoria della mia vita* (1945).
2. Miguel P. Corrales, *Ceramics, Tuna-Fisheries and Copper Mines; Salamandra* #8/9, Madrid 1997-98, see pp. 15-25 in this volume. Also José Manuel Rojo, *The Sound of Chains – the gothic sentiment within industrial archaeology; Salamandra* #10, 1999, see pp. 26-37 in this volume.
3. As if one could hear or feel the vegetation live and the "soul of nature" whisper. Certain Scandinavian so called national romantics around 1900 have in their best moments constituted a kind of rural equivalent to De Chirico, as if they intuitively understood and tried to find their way back to those roots that belong to ancient poetry when the earth was still very sparsely populated.
4. "The dominating tendency of mental life, and perhaps of neurological life in general, is the effort to reduce, to keep constant or to remove internal tension due to stimuli (the "Nirvana principle" to borrow a term from Barbara Low) – a tendency which finds expression

in the pleasure principle, and our recognition of that fact is one of our strongest reasons for believing in the existence of death instincts." *Beyond the Pleasure Principle;* Sigmund Freud 1928.

5. A certain melancholy, a certain nostalgia and maybe even a certain exoticism that belong to such places have made it possible to utilise them for aesthetic, cultural purposes. Likewise, the interest of pre-romantics and romantics for ruins and certain landscapes can probably be said to have contributed to the rise of tourism (even if it is mainly a question of more spectacular places). It is then the impressive aspect of certain places – purely physical or also the knowledge of the place's special, for example historical role – that takes the upper hand and not unprejudically because of the place's own, often modest character. But we are leaving the subject here.

The somewhat naive, nocturnal milieus of Paul Delvaux which are encumbered with disturbing naked women and other irrelevant figures who totally ruin what could have been of a certain interest with these paintings.

Poetic Spaces

by Bruno Jacobs

Nothing stops with the individual.
The ego presents that strange property of being at one and the same time hermetic and porous.
– Paul Nougé

Which are the landscapes that have shaped us?

What do we expect from a place?

Certain places and the stubborn seriousness and intimacy of the objects and of nature – which incidentally does not exclude strong doses of an often dull humor – become a silent antipode of sorts, maybe even an insult against the spectacular, against the mediocre superficiality of mass media and easy entertainment.

The loneliness but radiance of objects and the "metaphysics" of the physical world are all phenomena that tend to become almost commonplace when one pays attention to them, as if these and a certain timeless dimension were an inherent part of objects and nature.

One of the most important critical and most significant tasks of the poetic spirit today is maybe to put this "immediacity" and its experience in opposition to *the cultural* and what could be called its out-distancing or artificiality. The life of the inorganic, the presence, mystery or "full emptiness" of objects, all possess a very healthy subversive function – an excellent point of departure.

Porous man, contrary to today's alienated and hyperactive ideal, ponders, seeks to partake of, and lets himself become imbued with the mute surroundings, with the specific risks and the chill that it implicates, rather than trying to command and subjugate them.

•

One of the main characteristic features of poetry has been said to be condensation. And isn't it also precisely this condensation that we sometimes perceive in certain places which we sometimes feel that we share common points of contact with, possibly connecting with more or less unconscious aspects of our minds?

We have here poetic perspectives that we know also involve other more or less bewildering values and that make us see with a changed perspective – or with eyes of stone, of wood or of water.

It is a variety of condensation that we recognize or have presentiments of from within our dreams in which the surroundings or landscapes can be experienced as being particularly charged. The same often applies to places as we remember them or think we remember them, and no less to places from childhood or those which have been influenced by childhood's mentality.

Such spaces may be more or less illusory or deformed, but sometimes we encounter specific correspondences to them in the present, in reality, *objectively* so to speak.
It is about a given, "ready made" poetry that is physical, sensual and for the most part, quiet, and which surpasses the conventional poem in its ability to invade us.

The more condensation the more poetic?

A sandy desert or the surface of the ocean – not to mention the sky – maybe are among the poetically most obvious places precisely because of their overwhelming simplicity.

•

> *It is said that, terrified when darkness fell, they went towards sunset, believing that daylight would never return.*
> – Statius; Thebaid IV, 282.

The myth from antiquity about the terrible loneliness of the first humans in the world actualizes the fact that beauty and a certain type of space and time related poetry (like the one evoked precisely by sunsets) can also be associated with horror and anguish, these motive forces in existence.

Thus we have the great experiences from the past to start with.

Certain places can be perceived as poetic for cultural reasons, because of references of poetic character, contaminating an otherwise scarcely remarkable place. Sometimes it can be a combination of different cultural aspects. Dodona in ancient Greece with its rustling oracular oaks or the ziggurats of Persia with their connection with the firmament, or the also ancient Greek and subsequently medieval "sidereal geography" – important buildings, temples, cathedrals or roads arranged according to the patterns of the starry sky or the Milky Way as in the case of the pilgrimage to Santiago de Compostella in northern Spain (1) – are but a few such examples. And today maybe these naked and prosaic lawns between the runways of airports – in their own way a reflection of our indigent times – that are always similar throughout the whole world and in a kind of silent communication with each other.

There are also locations – often insignificant ones – that obtain poetic qualities owing to a certain atmosphere, a certain mysteriousness or specific disquieting character. It can be desert places, tentatively labeled "metaphysical places" (2) or locations that are quite simply unusual, often in a subtle rather than manifest way.

Certain remote areas retain a poetic energy due to their geographic peculiarity – like Iceberg Alley west of Greenland and all the others that I don't need to mention – despite the fact that their diffuse and therefore imaginative side has been altered by their profitable media value.

Others get their poetic character from the contrast or conflict that emerges there: ruins in nature, or an urban environment when it has been invaded by wilderness, as is observed in many "worthless" places in cities (3).

Also, these environments have been poeticized by man by way of an added detail, a certain intervention or in a deliberate, thorough way. It is found, to start with, in the cave paintings of Altamira in Spain or Lascaux in France, among others, with a beauty that seems to be strengthened by their old age. Or even better, the secret rock paintings in northern Australia: in contrast to the prehistoric cave paintings from Europe and the Americas that remain at least partly enigmatic, there is still a living relationship among certain aboriginal groups with the sacral and significantly less naturalistic rock paintings so harmonically spread throughout the landscape, often in the open.

Additional poetic places have a more or less latent poetic side revealed or enhanced through lyric meditation, subjective projection or intense focused interpretation (4).

Finally, and maybe above everything else, these places manifest their poetic quality through references that engender, stage or manifest correspondences with the rocks, in the vegetation, in the air or in the surrounding light: places existing as physical analogies, maybe materializations in the space and time of a representation, a concept or an aspect of our mental life.

We investigate these kinds of places and maybe a few more like those locales that temporarily and sporadically become poetic, for a brief moment under certain circumstances, at a certain time of day or of the year, maybe solely in a particular type of weather or if precipitously abandoned – as if escaping prevailing time and space or contrarily, as crystallizations in the midst of the ordinary or the indigent.

Such spots can sometimes be dimly seen or discerned in the dark, within the interstices existing between rational understanding and the old idea that what isn't seen therefore doesn't exist *or almost:* a lack or an absence of the poetic kind.

What remains ultimately is the unpredictable thing *in itself.*

---

1. Guy René Doumayrou, *La géographie sidérale* (Paris, 1976).
2. Bruno Jacobs, *The presence of emptiness,* 2003, pp. 38-42 in this volume.
3. Or *atoposes.* The Surrealist Group in Stockholm dedicated itself in the late 1990's at the study of various types of such "worthless" places. See also Miguel P. Corrales' text published here in English translation.
4. See for example Eugenio Castro *En la montaña del Torcal – Sésamo multiplicado,* Madrid, 1997, or the interpretation of an island in the Stockholm archipelago during a one day expedition by members of the Surrealist Group in Stockholm in 1999, *Lucifer,* Stockholm 2000.

Addendum

As the meeting point of the sky, of the sea and of the earth – the imperceptible persists of the old marine salt, that memory of the waves. The *Salina Tres Amigos,* San Fernando (Cádiz) in Andalucía, southern Spain, is an abandoned saltwork along the highway, one among several similar ones that together cover a significant area around the Cádiz Bay. The Atlantic ocean can be perceived on the horizon behind the long shallow, sometimes partly dry basins, broken mirrors reflecting the fleeing clouds. On the right a stream flows with its odoriferous banks of black mud at low tide crowded by a myriad of small shy crabs.

The openness of this wide, discarded, empty zone on the edge of the ocean where nothing occurs except Time itself idling, is being enhanced by the nakedness of the "three friends" sky, sea and ochre colored earth, themselves imbued with the presence of an almost timeless time which thereby aquires a peculiar density in the breeze.

And the vanished salt with its ancient analogies, reminding us of oblivion itself, salt as a medium, strenghtening the deep sensation of the truly *central* quality of the place.

September 29th 2003

INA TRES AMIGOS RIO ARILLO

Baligan

by Guy Girard

I was born in and spent all of my childhood in Flamanville (*), on the west coast of that protruding peninsula shaped by the Cotentin. A road crosses the village from the north to the south from the northern part of la Hague that curves around to touch Aurigny, the nearest of the Channel Islands, and which goes down along the increasingly sandy coast until reaching the vast opening of the bay at the Mont-Saint-Michel.

The village area is enclosed in a bow whose rough curve is a granite cliff with three full kilometers of length that offered the most exemplary carvings of natural poetry as well as of the legends filled with traces of local history. Almost two decades ago, half of that cliff was destroyed, meticulously erased so as to make space for a nuclear power station. Earlier, for a century, what disturbed the goblins in their geological tribulations was the alternation of various activities and misfortunes of an underwater iron mine whose exploits ended definitively at the beginning of the sixties. The mine shaft, from the outset of the trail of the custom-house officers, its annex buildings of red bricks, as well as the miners' quarters situated away from the cliff, built like those in Flanders or in Lorraine, seemed to me like a desolate collage that demonstrates its charm only through the ruin of that enterprise, thanks to the patient vandalism of the children and of the sea breeze. A more ancient state of abandon had settled over the granite quarries, which under the ferns look like structures of medieval architecture. In the past, I was told that they provided many streets of Paris with paving stones. In order to believe this, I only need to pass Château-d'eau street, where a trace of the legend about the dragon that inhabited the Baligan Pit, a few hundred steps from the old mine, can be seen on the right sidewalk when going towards Faubourg-Saint-Denis street.

In mythical times, the monster had the villagers ritually delivering some of their children to it. This lasted until Germain Scot, the future patron of the parish who came from Ireland in a vessel shaped like a wheel, cleared the area of this plague only to impose another one:

the christian religion. He is said to have killed the beast after having tied it up with his stole, either by drowning it in a deep pond close to the cavern, known as the Citerne, or by transforming it into a rock – a huge block of granite veined red by the blood of the victims and which served to build the dyke at the port of Flamanville, Diélette, during the last century. In addition to these red markings, one can also notice prints similar to children's footprints on the rocks and stones along the seashore near Trou Baligan, and which I look for on the Parisian pavements.

These telluric forces are further emphasized at the edge of the cape, behind the semaphore, by a dolmen made of stones of ovoid shape, the Pierre au Rey which is spelled by others as Pierre Aurée. On the top stone are some engraved characters of an undeciphered but rune-like writing, as well as a human profile with a very long nose. Even if this dolmen is the only duly registered megalithic monument in the entire municipality, piles of stones are still found on the cliff and in the fields along it, arrayed with such geometrical rigour, which in my opinion demonstrates human intent. Placed in this way as guardians of a certain meaning or as the seeds of fertile images, I am puzzled when approaching their secret in a dream: thus one night in the fall of 1980, while walking near the semaphore, I notice that one of the heavy stones with the semblance of a short menhir in the nearby field has been toppled, leaving a large hole at its base: the entrance of an underground passage, or perhaps an ancient funeral chamber. I jump in only to find myself in front of a skeletal guardian of treasure from the Gallic epoch. Frightened, I flee through the passage which, during my flight, changes into a passage of the Parisian catacombs where I meet Breton and Aragon as they had looked in the twenties.

If these were the hosts of a dream that I had in Flamanville the night after having walked in that somewhat upside-down field, I was lead to discover that many surrealists, without conferring with each other, also came to that village. First there were Claude Tarnaud, Alain Jouffroy and a young couple whose identity still escapes me, in May 1948, as I learned from reading the first issue of the journal *Supérieur inconnu*. In a letter to Sarane Alexandrian, Tarnaud gave an account of the initiatic character of the place:

"I believe that I found here several series of KEYS that (acting, I know it, in the very center of what I would call my "personal myth") still

leave me very perplexed regarding which doors they open. For example at the entrance of the Baligan pit – a giant fault that sinks almost two hundred meters into the ground – the sumptuous mouth, as that of a nave, at first sight with walls deliberately PAINTED with large bloody stains (rust is responsible; the rock here is iron ore) – a hall completely blocked by an enormous rock shaped like the top of a lance marked at the tip with the symbol of Saturn drawn by the very veins of the rock. That point (I was the Only One, due to my well-known slimness, to manage with great effort to insert myself in that hall) was aimed directly at a sleeping bat balancing from the wall like an enormous shell supported by two fragments of pink seaweed (…)."

This Saturnian character was also perceived by the Prague surrealist Ivo Purs who in the summer of 1994, while staying in a nearby village, went to the cliff where he discovered the "tooth of Saturn" in one of the natural megaliths. In the meantime, Jean-Pierre Guillon, Josette Exandier, Roger Renaud, and Michel Zimbacca passed through. Finally Thomas Mordant informed me that he went there now and then, sometimes together with Ody Saban, staying in the house that his grandfather, of Belgian origin like him, had bought as a summer house. If one leaves the strictly municipal area and takes a look at La Hague, it appears that Max Bucaille was born in that district and that Jacques Prévert spent his last years there, after having discovered this landscape in the 20's during a summer trip with some friends and Yves Tanguy.

Marie-Dominique Massoni goes there every year with her companion Jean-Jacques Méric, who had been found again by an old friend who had returned from Hong-Kong and who had infused new life to his family mansion, Urville-Nacqueville, over the years. Not far away, in Gréville, is painter Jean-François Millet's birth house that Salvador Dali visited in 1971. In Cherbourg (apart from the fact that it is there that Breton embarked for Mexico and where I met the granddaughter of Douanier Rousseau in the company of a friend to whom she gave a few piano lessons), Georges Izambard was teaching there when he received a letter from Rimbaud. Oppositely, to the west, Jersey welcomed Claude Cahun after Victor Hugo who preferred Guernesey to the former.

If we are dealing here with a charm peculiar to these places which during legendary times worked under the flight of a dragon and which nowadays is manifested within this constellation of encounters, I expect it to show me more than the first landmark of a quest, but instead a trajectory and a movement initiated with the agility of rabbits that run through the moorland where the wheels of fire of the chthonian site were rolling down towards different starry sites. The landscapes, one inside the other. In the morning of April 28th 1994 I had the following dream: I am running at full speed on the highway that crosses my village in the direction where the setting sun is disappearing. As if that disappearance was definitive, I invent or recall fragments of ancient knowledge, incantations from ancient Egypt to Amon-Râ. Without loosing any breath, I shout the semblance of a litany that might as well be a call for the presence of Osiris whose dismembered body perhaps floats in the clouds that invade the sky. Then I have to invoke Isis after shortly seeing the effect of my words. On the side of the road, a long series of objects made of white stone are erected which, as I instantly know, are hieroglyphs engraved in three dimensions designed to record the eagerness of my words.

What about taking that road now? As it exists in real space (in the dream it was flanked by black hedges and coming from the west) it passes in front of the Jean-Jacques tower, an octogonal tower that the marquis of Sesmaisons, lord of Flamanville, had built in the XVIII century for Jean-Jacques Rousseau who never went there. If it fascinated me as a child during nights of festivities that were lit with fireworks, it frightened me more often when I imagined it being haunted by a ghost covered with ivy like the one on the facade that at the time had perpetually closed shutters, which to me was the totally unknown Jean-Jacques. Later, when discovering Paris, and by way of a homophonic association, I compared it to the Saint-Jacques tower. Like the latter, perhaps it marks the beginning of a quest. In Flamanville, situated on the road at the end of the lane that leads to the family home, for me it separates the north from the south. My original attraction to the north was consummated through a friendly meeting with young icelandic surrealists in the beginning of the 80's. It was in 1983 that I discovered Barcelona in the company of one of them, Olafur Engilbertsson who lived there. A line can be drawn on a map of Europe that unites Flamanville and Barcelona; extended north, it reaches Iceland, and south first the Mont Saint-Michel island and, before reaching Barcelona, the sacred mountain of Montserrat whose monasterial library contains many Egyptian antiquities among which a painting on a sarcophagus depicts the eyes of Horus. Further across the sea it meets Mallorca. How many dragons roam that trajectory? The effigy of one of them, as they appear in the popular festivals of Catalonia, was given to me as a present or talisman two years ago on the occasion of her first visit to Paris by the woman whom I loved at the time and who is now living in Barcelona.

Tuesday June 22th 1999

(*) on the northwestern coast of France. Translator's note.

Garraf

by Manuel Crespo

1

The earth's poetry never ceases.
– John Keats

We won't let them remove the part of nature contained in us.
We won't lose even a stamen of it, we won't cede even a pebble from its water.
– René Char

Perhaps sight is the most appropriate sense for exploring the real. But modern humans suffer from deteriorating vision. The more that the supply of images has proliferated, that they have lost substance and weight, we've suffered from a progressive narrowing of the angle of vision, arriving at the characteristic plainness of the visible as it is today. The relation of the pupil with the horizon, with the external, is poor, since many visual sensations and vital experiences are now distinct, and are lived vicariously from the spectator's seat which has been assigned to all of us, and from which it's difficult to leave behind. Also contributing to our passivity is the minimal opportunity for connecting with our natural surroundings, especially if they don't correspond with the promotional images of travel agencies, if their mediocre appearance isn't suitable for promoting as a vacation destination or for rushed visits, during those negligible periods which work allots to relaxation. Earn a living: what a sad phrase.

We have so little time that our modest outskirts aren't enough. At the very least, our money should provide us with a spectacular view.

Like adolescents with their bodies, our current relationship with images is bulimic. We devour them voraciously, expel them with disgust, and they leave an enervating emptiness in our retinas.

This apathy is an aspect of the social trend that accepts the given as the best of possible circumstances. Not in vain has a pessimistic discourse been implanted in the western psyche according to which we're mere epigones, inhabitants of a terminal epoch with our eyes wide open to the disasters provoked by technology and a vengeful earth, and closed to the loving contemplation of the revelations that occur daily and contain a convulsive power. The "quotidian magic" which Breton spoke of.

Nevertheless, if there's one human activity that has kept its prestige intact, and that preserves the principles of freedom within itself, it's wandering aimlessly with no purpose, letting oneself go, yielding to impulse and the hope of chance encounters. Whoever has once ventured down deserted streets in pursuit of the ephemeral; or through the weeds and refuse of derelict lots, simply in order to evoke childhood and the games that with the passing of time acquire a tragic solemnity; whoever has ambled along sandy beaches in winter, just because they heard someone call from the breakwater, corroborated by footprints leading nowhere or who have been captivated by clusters of seashells reminiscent of the constellations, has felt the pleasure of controlling their own time, without worrying about its usefulness. At some point, *they saw*, discovered its treasures.

We preserve the wild substance, undoubtedly emanating from the nucleus of every cell, that links us to nature, to the life which unfolds like a familiar and persistent melody shared among the living – and which everything, even the inanimate, breathes. A melody connects them: "Silly refrains, naïve rhythms" (Rimbaud) of the seasons, linked together by infinite, and hence extremely fertile, sequences, of variations on the same theme.

"Randomly scattered refuse, the world's most beautiful order," wrote Heraclitus of Ephesus, an opinion that today has acquired the precision of an hypothesis.

Scientific theories like that of Gaia, always belated with respect to poetic intuitions, view the planet's surface not as what makes life possible, but as an indivisible part of it; and the mantle of air, the troposphere, as its circulatory system. According to Lovelock's so-called "Daisy World," a mathematical model that posits a simple planet populated by black and white daisies that grow at different temperatures and are heated by continuously increasing thermal radiation, it's clear that the system is autoregulated as a consequence of retro-alimentary loops between the organisms and their environment. Hence, it's now understood that everything, including humans, constantly interact. Nobody nor anything is immune to the perpetual ebb and flow that constitutes the milieu to which life adapts itself.

Moreover, human beings go beyond this adapting: they imagine, anticipate; a will to perfection prefigures their actions. They perceive the external as porous, as a process which they can influence. The key is how to use that impulse.

To wander among rocks, roam the streets of deserted neighborhoods, contemplate the view from a precipice, foster a trust that merges with the landscape by means of desire, of an a-rational affectivity against which the personality, that outer varnish which aspires to uniqueness, normally protects itself, creating an atmosphere favorable to the advent of the not-yet-been that without remembering it becomes familiar with, and which is hidden, although "on the tip of the tongue"; which burns inside and which seems on the verge of tangibility and whose emblems are chance and coincidence, slippages of phenomena that are not at all as random as they might seem at first, since it's the singular way that the minds of our epoch position themselves when they arise which confers on them their peculiar nature.

For my part, I can say I'm familiar with these decisive moments, which possess, moreover, the nostalgia of the incommunicable, in which things seem to shine and want to leave their places, but this is not the result of some talent superior to others', because I know they're the patrimony of everyone. It's enough to have been a child. During a run-of-the-mill maturity, you have to force the crisis by means of a *hunger* that leads to rebellion and curiosity, and it's necessary to oppose a reality diminished by habit and which is largely absurd and always cruel, with that other Reality in which the conceivable and still utopian, as well as the ungovernable, also participate, since strangely enough that's what corresponds to us, and whom it seems to exclusively address, while denying the superstitious certainty with which we confront our destiny.

I don't mean to highlight the possible analogies and symbolic interpretations provoked by such things, however, beyond the obvious ones, which I also haven't tried to avoid, without wishing to limit their meaning and dynamism, but rather depict then. I seek asepsis in both writing and photography, and use the camera as a verification tool. Though I'm not fooling myself, either: the weight of aesthetic culture and education doesn't always make this possible.

"If I still have a taste for anything / it's for the earth and stones,"

Rimbaud says in his poem, "Revelries of Hunger." The message of these lines by the clairvoyant poet *par excellence*, who like few others intuited the alienation of the best part of the human animal subjected to massive proletariatization and the ubiquity of the market economy, which at that time was dawning and now has reached paroxysm, cries out today with urgency.

Yes, it's now imperative: faced with the virtual and the insipid, we have to embrace the direct and sensual, assure ourselves that "*this exits*," beyond what can be proven empirically; we have to grab hold of some certainty as yet unrestrained. Retake, though it might seem modest, the elemental tack that sophisticated procedures evade, perhaps to conceal their dullness, or malevolence.

The Catalan region of Garraf doesn't have any particular attributes that make it stand out with respect to any other benefiting from the Mediterranean littoral and a number of hills, austere in both aspect and vegetation.

The sea delimits the area, and behind it rise massive limestone cliffs, ascending to the barren and severely eroded plain; it's a desolate landscape whose perimeter is defined by the horizon, punctuated by a few twisted pines, aromatic plants, pita, lentisco and palmettos that grip the stony and unstable ground, in whose subsoil arroyos and caverns form, and from which spring whistles and echoings of wind, which frequently play among the crevices and gorges.

It's a solitary spot, settled in the past by sporadic human communities, which one senses were populated by adventurers, inveterate failures and sentries assigned to rudimentary outlooks on the watch for pirates that for centuries harassed the coast hereabouts; individuals marked by the ruggedness of a terrain they had to face with courage.

For lack of written records, legends and vague proverbs circulate throughout the Garraf region, including paranormal episodes occurring on the Pleta homestead, where I once had to escape from a swarm of bees that only attacked those who got too near the abandoned house.

There are rumors of passionate crimes, and gruesome corpses are sometimes discovered in the ravines, where they'd been thrown in hopes that they would never be found.

This mythic humus contributes to the chill of the enigmatic felt by the explorer. I've confirmed the attraction experienced by those who wander here. It seems that legends infuse the place.

The fact is that it's easy to suffer the allure of this region—I say suffer because such intensity contains something fatal, compulsory—evidenced at times by the pressure to go there which gradually overcomes me.

I've become accustomed to Garraf through my window. There are times when I don't look at it, but I know it's there, and I feel it *looking back*, as absurd as that might seem. And then I have to respond, not only to the scars produced by the quarries and land speculation that exploit it, but also to the sinuosity of its hills, dotted with pines; to the flocks of seagulls, their soaring guided by an instinctive resolve; to the storm clouds hovering over the mountaintops and the falling stars, that on summer nights drop from the firmament. The wonders which arise are mine, magnets of revelation, neither static nor ecstatic, but alive to adventure.

The approach is by a steep road. One's gaze is ensnared by the mass of sea, which expands remarkably as you ascend, so that from the heights one perceives a vastness lacking in the view from the shoreline. The Mediterranean is an enormous sleeping body that breathes.

The chasms crossed by the path have something of the initiatic, of dangers to be navigated in order to arrive at the plateau, inaugurated by a small wood, where it's pleasant to pause.

In contrast with the silence of the spot, the barking of hundreds of dogs is terrifying to the point of paralysis. There's an animal refuge in the vicinity; and a cemetery. As I make my way forward, the stridency increases to an unbearable degree, and fear overpowers ambition. Behind the densely built fence I can see their fierce jaws and I quickly flee. Perturbed, I turn to the left toward the center of the pinewood, walking among thickets from which buzzings escape.

It's a clearing, overlooking the littoral, and someone has placed a branch that looks like goat antlers stuck in a pile of rocks. There are liquor and beer bottles lying around.

What ceremony was celebrated here?

The color of the vegetation is dun and pale green. Defensive thorns are common, due to an aridity that increases the sound of snapping branches as some animal bolts swiftly away upon hearing my

approaching footsteps. Perhaps it adds to the sharpening of the feeling: suddenly, the future seems ready to resolve itself into a providential or fateful instant.

A large snake passes dizzyingly by me. It's impossible to photograph. The wind, blowing at my back, whispers syllables, lulls, slanders. More than human, it seems like some superhuman pleased with the perplexity. The pitas are frequently injured, plucked by sparrows or small birds of prey, perhaps gnawed by animals. Some marks are curiously reminiscent of insects perched on their leaves: their negatives or a tattoo.

The cumulous and lavender cirrus mark the highest point, Rascler Peak. Ferns invade the edges of the path in a confirmation of their supremacy and perseverance; they gather together in a lyrical and perfectly haphazard jumble.

The full moon is visible at noon.

Space is unaccustomedly ample. It opens to the world.

To the right, I discover a rocky, dusty trail that I'd never noticed before. It enters a bramble patch and disappears.

In the distance I spot the ruins of a circular wall just above the high tide line. The beauty of the setting with its tower is remarkable: the gracefulness of the walls, built with a technique which takes advantage of the rough edges of the irregular stones, joined without the use of any bonding agent. They effortlessly support each other's weight. And their placement is certainly not at the most strategic point, nor does it offer wide views, but is a simple nook, protected from the wind and so silent, where they must have passed languid hours, spent dozing idly, daydreaming and fantasizing; in frugal meals, confidences, and gossip, interrupted sometimes by the terrible surprise of enemy sails and the anguish of knowing that the future depended on the accurate emission and interpretation of certain signals before the imminent danger.

2

It's been recovered!
What? Eternity.
It's the sea united
With the sun.
– Rimbaud.

THE CORDS, stiff with sea water:
The large
white knot – this time,
doesn't come undone.
– Paul Celan

Humility and simplicity are privileges of the authentic. There, exposed to the elements, mystery likes to show itself.

Solitude and certain sensitive energies in the echo of footsteps, the cats which flee when we draw near, the jangling of the sailboats' masts in the harbor, the sidereal accumulation of seashells, the derelict train station, of exaggerated opulence for a token stop, where hardly a local train ever frequents, indicate during certain suggestive interludes, the crucial hour in which the surroundings seem to grow, the mute begins to mumble and objects give up resisting.

It seems useless to hold out, and its preferable to adopt the frame of mind of the bride in St John of the Cross' *Spiritual Canticle*: "you will say that I am lost; / that, stricken by love, / I lost myself, and was found."

So we're given over to the interstitial realm, to multiple fissures, to generally unnoticed vestiges. We await something different, a promise of improvement. What occurs after this moment is transcendent, though its message is unprecedented, but the conjecture about its value is redoubled internally, until it achieves certainty: it's life, in its immediacy and playful happiness: the truly absent life.

Where the sheer cliff wall falls into the waves there form small coves with rotund names like *Cala Morisca* (Moor's Cove), or *Del home mort* (Dead Man's Cove); or the area between *Pas de la mala dona* (Evil Woman Way) and *Punta dels Corrals* (Corral Point) where the white village of Garraf is located.

The small size of the village, and its relative obscurity—there's only one hotel, of dubious comfort, which is closed in winter—makes the place a summer residence for families who through inheritance enjoy their "*botigas*": wooden houses painted green and white, which front the sickle-shaped beach.

In off-season few dare make their residence here, despite its charm. The precariousness of public transport, the lack of services, the

icy dampness and the constant strong winds that cause frequent blackouts dissuade them.

Social life, moreover, is scarce.

There's just one bar and bistro, decrepit and enchanting, and a restaurant with gastronomic pretensions. The houses don't exceed three stories. The majority of them face the Mediterranean.

From this description it's easy to deduce that strolling around Garraf in the autumn, from the height of its main square down to the dunes, encourages one to attend to the presentiments that the slow pace illuminates; "mysterious exchanges between the physical and the mental" (Breton) which the gradations of light, so variable along the coast, and the shimmering of the sun when it rubs the crests of waves, must approach.

To reach Garraf by road, you have to pass the railway tunnel, and leave behind a hallucinatory art nouveau mansion built by Gaudí beside the ruins of a defensive tower. Once again this fear of the other, which sails toward misfortune, the death which comes from the nocturnal sea; as well as the novelty of a force which bears the otherness that separates, before which they erected a stage set which at heart is useless, because these defensive works are better explained as a curiosity about the foreign rather than for their pretended function as impregnable bastions.

Clearing the pass is reminiscent of overcoming some test intended to alter the conscience, to prepare it for the new. The transition from a work of engineering—asphalt, concrete, stoplight—to the wild is remarkable. From the shadowy side, to the luminous outside of plaster and the expanded sky. It's no longer just a physical transition, but a movement toward the yearned-for intensity: dawn.

The walk begins at the highest point, where the view of the mountain is complete. It rises above the rooftops and imprisons the houses.

The train tracks, moreover, cut across the path. Claustrophobia drives us in a single direction, which circles the buildings from behind. It's a gradual descent to the waters, gleaming and rhythmic, which are fed by the subterranean springs that emerge here, like that of *La Falconera*, whose black arch is sunk in the rock and whose course remains unexplored.

From the presence of humans and their constructions, to their

absence, like plunging into the lakes of the unconscious. And it's true that, as we walk, fascination helps restricted reason (for which everything is rational) to escape; and an opaque logic begins to connect what we encounter with oneiric cadences; from pleasure as well as necessity.

It's a joy to let oneself go. To witness, participate in the destruction of reality by a recreated world. It's understood, emotionally, that we still have a long way to go, that the assault of certain phenomena, once ordinary and now important transmission mecanisms, transform us. It's the seminal moment in which existence shakes off its sad patina.

I amble along the docks and boat slips, pausing before some flowers and cacti, diving with my heart into the current. I cross the breakwater, and my feet have to adapt themselves to the blocks arrayed to stem the tides, recuperating an ancestral, nearly atrophied function. Some cold local wind that doesn't stop blowing, *el Ponent*, *el Garbí*, stirs my hair, rubs my ears, makes my eyes water.

The spirit is predisposed to magic, gives it *carte blanche*. On the roof of one of the port buildings, visible from the street, someone has casually tossed a length of rope. Its similarity to the outlines of a salamander surprises me, so similar that it recalls the logotype of a certain literary magazine.

Strange impulses lead me to the beach. The pulse and heartbeat keep time with each experience. I decide quickly. Things flash, and I don't want to miss a thing. There's an arrow drawn in the asphalt. I force myself to follow it. I have to descend some twisted spiral stairs. I see a damaged wall, the gray cement that caused the plaster to fall makes me think of an underground world, one looming behind appearances. There's a red cross painted on the wall. Red alert.

A small circular area, incongruent, about three hands high, which must have had some function for some now unused food stall, is paired with a rampart that I photographed sometime before. Beside the opening I find a piece of woman's scarlet underwear and a rusty door retaining a stone marker painted with the colors of the rainbow and a partially erased inscription: "ito." Nearby, the labels of a brand of ice cream on a closed stall, of which the syllables "igo" and "go" are all that's legible.

A dog comes to greet me. He's curious about my photographic labors. I squat down to his level. He examines my extended hand. We establish a mutual sympathy. He briefly explores the house porches. He sniffs me, then goes away.

Some hundred meters away, in the middle of the beach, I spot a plastic dog that someone has placed on a small pedestal.

Some rock formations persist in their peculiar postures, the erosion of saltwater unsuccessful in defeating their extravagant desire for uniqueness. Like all immemorial things, they are anxious to offer the remains of darkness, ancient preconscious states, mutterings previous to language.

Towards the east, the closed hotel and bar suggest ruins of buried civilizations, decadent monuments. There is some offensive, untranslatable graffiti, turbid scrawls, tin cans, ash from fires, paper, weeds, an indistinct phrase that lends its name to the improvised dump: "Bay of Pigs."

From the other side, I look for the green flash in the afternoon's silvery veil, which glimmers on the metal. Beams of golden and bluish light glide among the pebbles, which absorb them and metamorphose into jewels, the shells into coins; beams that illuminate the pair of whales, drawn on the wall with a certain gracefulness, who draw their lips near to one another. One of them asks, and the other responds: "Yes."

The Poetic Scars of Obsolescence

by Eric W. Bragg

When an industrialized society no longer has any use for a building or cluster of buildings, the structures are sealed, thereby pushed into a new dimension which prepares them for some of the most wondrous transformations. After a layer of dust has settled there, and nature has once again asserted itself by way of intrusive plantlife, the edifice has been transformed: try as the property owners might to keep the entrances boarded, the structure still manages to attract the attention of the young and the curious, the homeless and the explorers. The battle over the place ensues: one day a plywood board is placed over an opened window or entranceway, while the next, the board is removed by someone else. And from these visitations by all manner of folk who are not part of the mainstream, there accumulate poetic memories, spray-painted messages and the most peculiar sorts of discarded objects. The contradiction between what the building was (and what it represented) versus what it has become has the potential to inspire within the visitor the entire spectrum of emotions.

By way of terminology, the Californian "ruins" described in this article are mostly the remains of urban buildings and dwellings. The majority of them are fairly recent, in that they have been abandoned to the elements for only a few decades. The abandoned ruins in California are very modern, with relatively little history, when compared with ruins found in Europe, for example. Despite their relative youth, the locations documented here certainly have their share of interesting artifacts, entropic processes of nature and other mysteries of the interactive, collective unconscious.

In recent years, the term "urban exploration" has surfaced. For some, the justification of urban exploration resides in the thrill of transgression, of breaking the rules of forbiddeness defined by the state, of disregarding the arbitrary law of private property. For others, it is the thrill of physical danger in dark places, such as exploring active subway tracks. Still there are some who enjoy bringing their lover to an abandoned site just for romantic purposes. Apparently there are many varieties of pleasure that appeal to these individuals who explore the ruined buildings of urban life. With the rise of the internet and subsequent mass-availability of digital photography, this obsessive activity known as "urban exploration" has mushroomed over the past few years.

While these various "thrills" and pleasures of urban exploration certainly have their merits, the primary focus of this article is to document the gothic dimension of urban ruins in a surrealist capacity (with this gothic concept so well described by José Manuel Rojo in *The Gothic Sentiment within Industrial Archaeology*), meaning that this gothic sensibility is created by the collective psyche of all those who visit the urban ruin and interact with and transform its constitutive elements. In this respect, urban exploration has the opportunity to acquire a *surrealist dimension*, such that the ruins, and the found and vandalized objects within these environments, are considered to be *objects of desire*, and *objects of haunting,* thereby having the potential *to transform the way we perceive reality*. These poetic spaces and objects are special because they influence all those who encounter them, and simultaneously, they are transformed by the subversive hands of those who find them in the solitude of social neglect, *when no one is looking*.

From the gothic standpoint, many of these ruins initiate a questioning of the permanence and future of industrialism, an environmentally toxic and homicidal process first set into motion by capitalism and its derivative regimes (such as the "communist" dictatorships). Images of crumbling buildings, mutating offices, and long-disrupted places of manual labor suggest the ephemeral nature of alienated labor and private property, much to the disappointment of so many terrified, conservative minds. In their own special, haunting way, these places poetically measure the pulse of any culture by framing the current period of industrial stagnation (and capitalist decline, in many countries) in a way suggesting that the "civilized" human must evolve in more non-destructive ways.

Dialectically, the pursuit of urban exploration yields traces of the poetically defused remains from previous eras, previous regimes. Through the concept of historical materialism we can appreciate this dialectic: poetic artifacts from a finished era that have the potential to serve as analogical transformations of that culture's manner of thought, in the way an irritating grain of sand within an oyster is eventually transformed into a resplendent pearl. That these magical findings sometimes have an air of the gloomy and the sinister should not in any way depreciate their poetic value, and especially in the "gothic" sense, these gloomy and sinister qualities only suggest that the ruins are haunted by subjective ghosts of past oppression and tyranny. The forces of disrespect, exploitation and persecution are reduced to roaming ghosts that populate the lonely hallways. A terrible institution becomes a teetering shadow of its former self. Institutions of terror are immobilized by their own forgetfulness, with the permanent scars of obsolescence.

In California, these *scars of obsolescence* are plentiful as they are scattered over much terrain. In particular, there are many sites which remind us of past militarization, such as Angel Island, located just north of San Francisco in San Francisco Bay. During both the nineteenth and twentieth centuries, the island served as a place of militarization and persecution: from the American Civil War, to World War 1, to World War 2 (where German and Japanese prisoners of war were held), to the installation of anti-missile launchers during the cold-war era, Angel Island has been a place of violence. Now the island is touted by conservative historians as an "Ellis Island" of the Pacific coast, in order to inspire patriotic sentiment. Sprawling across the island are many of these militaristic ruins: defensive outposts, barracks, communal areas, hospitals. Some of these places have been recuperated in order to reify American concepts of patriotism, but there are many others which are still left alone to rot in their own decay as well as in the shame of their own horrible existence.

One of these very potent areas on the island is the now skeletal, concrete barracks located at Fort McDowell, on the eastern side of the island amid the decaying hospital, mess hall, and "Post Exchange." Close to the barracks are the engineering buildings with overgrown trees pushing through the spaces within concrete picnic benches. The barracks themselves are now all but gutted, with only a few traces of what used to exist there: old fuses, rusted tools, broken windows, shattered toilets and very little else. In the more inaccessible part of the building, I ascended a creepy staircase lined with peeling paint and daylight, as if I were being summoned to the upper mysteries of the unsettled building. In one of the bunk rooms on the uppermost floor, amid the littering

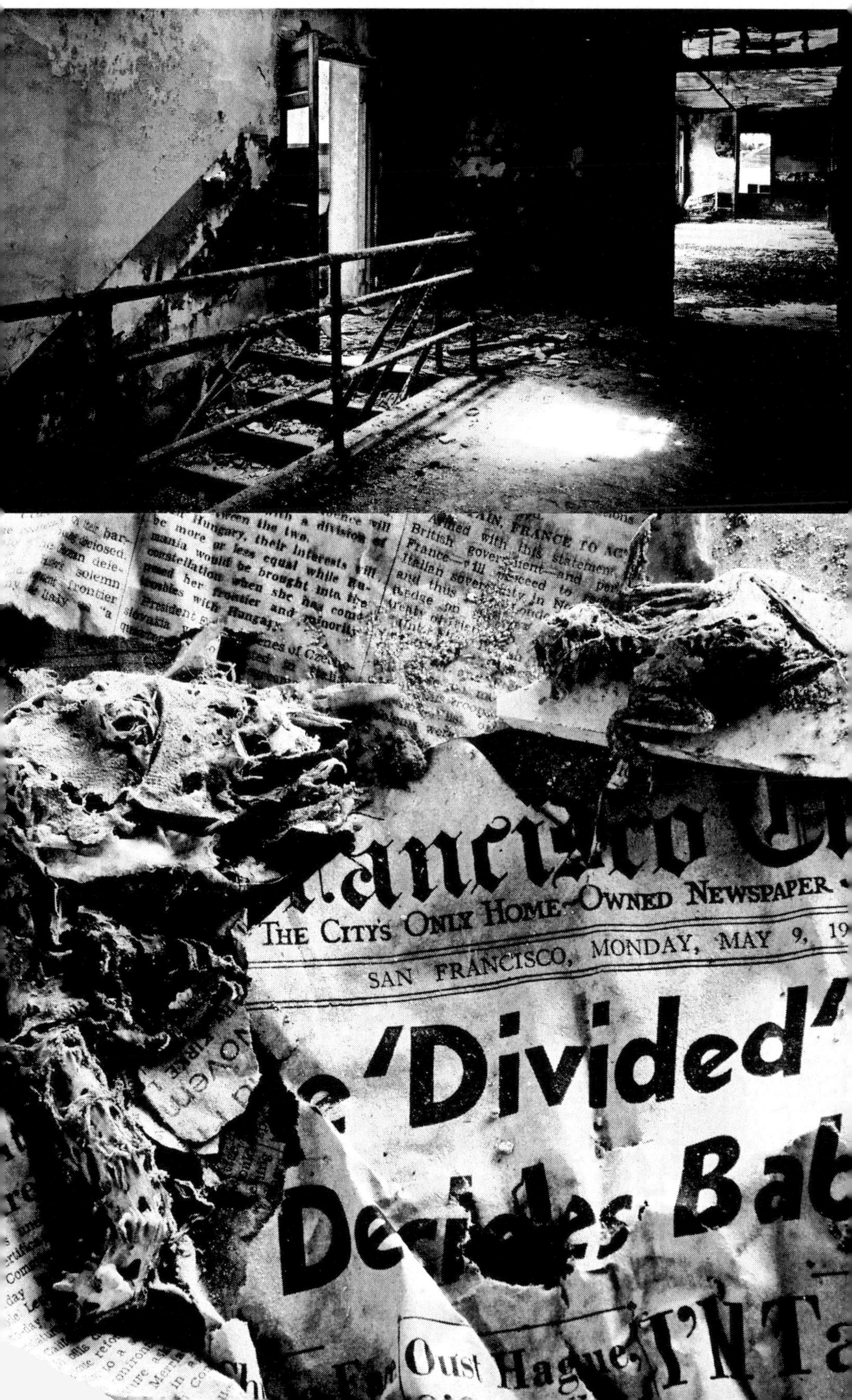
THE CITY'S ONLY HOME-OWNED NEWSPAPER
SAN FRANCISCO, MONDAY, MAY 9, 19
'Divided'
Oust Hague

flakes of paint and other debris blown about by wild gusts through the open, frameless windows, I found a pair of bird mummies, one big and one small, near a crumbling, yellowed newspaper from Monday, May 9, 1938, on which the headline word "divided" blared. This kind of poetic truth couldn't have been more obvious, but no less powerful.

While the Angel Island ruins speak greatly of nationalist aggression, the powerplant offered more of a domestic face to capitalist violence (and quite similar to the appeal of abandoned factories). Located in the eastern part of San Francisco, in a rundown industrial area, this powerplant looked as though it had been abandoned for decades. On the morning I went there, it was possible to see a large, solitary smokestack looming in the distance, vomiting smoke. As oppressive as that might have seemed, it was only when finding inside of the facility a dried artichoke next to a pair of sprouting potatoes that I realized that this area must have been very similar to the location that inspired DeChirico's painting entitled "The Conquest of the Philosopher."

Of the decrepit facilities themselves, they were in a great state of decay, with all metal fixtures rusted, with vandalized and spraypainted concrete. The ceiling windows of the main room (at least a majestic three storeys tall) had been broken out long ago, revealing a skeletal window framework that allowed the dazzling sunlight to illuminate the crumbling pipes of what must have been part of a steam generator. Ironically enough, the other corridors and rooms within this powerplant were without electricity, necessitating the use of a flashlight. And in some cases, some of the steps on the metal staircases had rusted away, creating a slightly hazardous but no less fascinating tour of a gritty industrial area whose lights had long since gone out. On the uppermost floor, the path to the control room was easy enough to find. The dials and knobs from the power regulation machinery had been removed, with plenty of graffiti left behind in their place. In the other, better lit parts of the powerplant, there were small weeds steadily gaining their foothold in the patches of sunlight.

The "invasion" of nature upon ruined buildings has its own obsessive appeal, perhaps reminding us of our mortality. Of course another way to consider this action is that nature is simply reclaiming what humans have tried to separate from it; in fact it was humanity's idea of considering itself separate from nature, so then

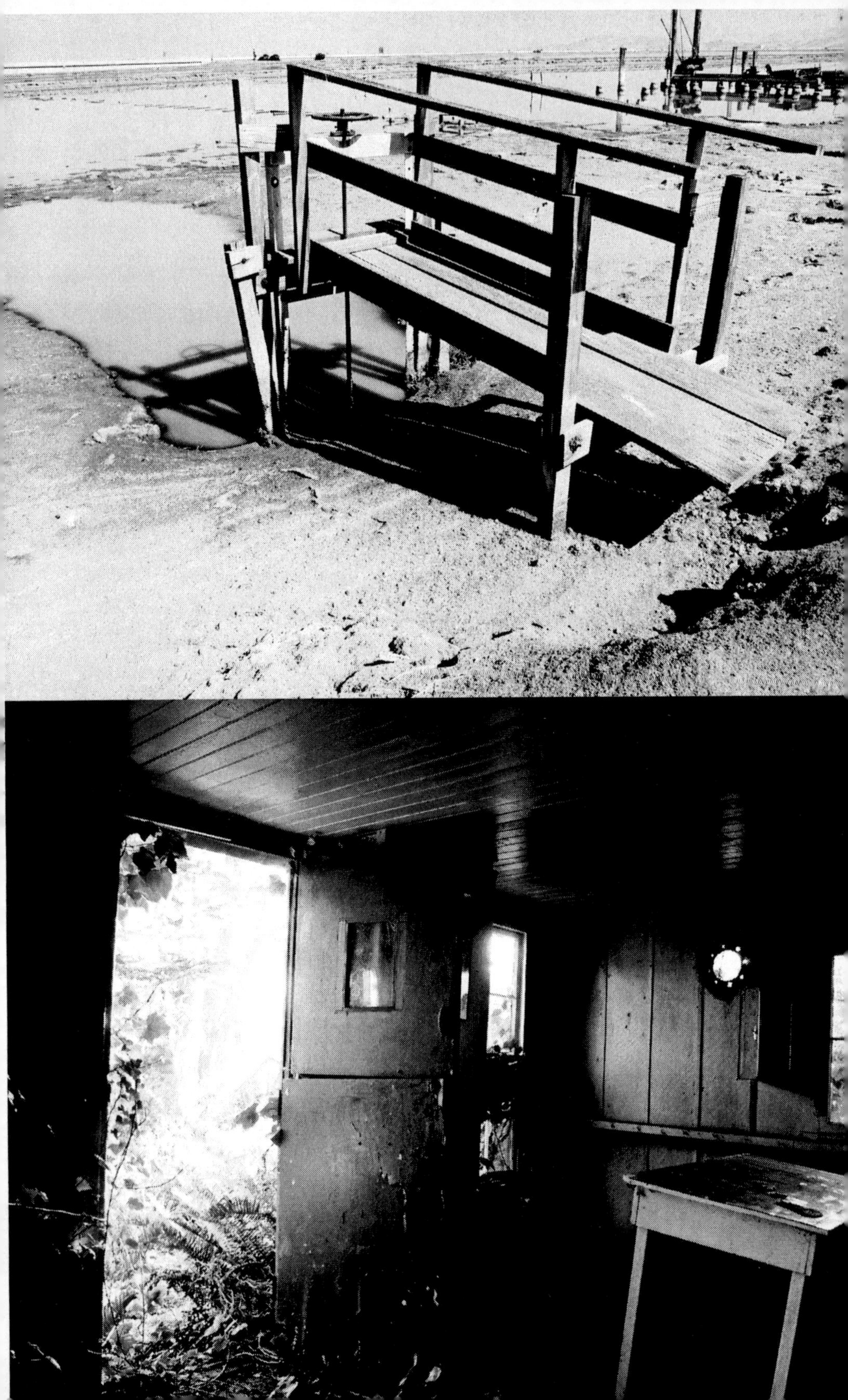

the reclamation of areas once exclusively controlled by humans will reveal this fallacy of thought. The small cottages choked with ivy near San Gregorio demonstrate this trend, as do some of the saltwork ruins found in the Newark area, close to the Dumbarton Bridge. Human spaces that have been slowly ravished and then converted by the elements have the tendency to become strongly poetic.

Another such place is the hotel resort spa in Byron, east of San Francisco Bay. Originally the hotel was frequented by celebrities and movie stars in the years before the second world war, but during the war it was used by the federal government as a secret location for the interrogation of captured German and Japanese soldiers. After the war the hotel and its grounds were used for a few years by a monastery, but subsequently, the area was left to ruin. The crumbling hotel is located on dried hills studded with the remnants of a palm forest which used to create the illusion of a paradise hideaway for the rich. Now the palms are either dead or overgrown, and the hotel has been falling apart due to the actions of both time and the vandalistic interventions of local youth. But the spirit of the place is captivating, with its numerous rooms and lost scenery, in a deliriously hot and dry environment. Next to one of the side buildings, I found a desiccated cow on its side, in a well-preserved state of mummification, with its front leg having been gnawed by some hungry animal. Next to this partially eaten leg was found a crutch, placed there most likely in a spirit of savage humor that could only exist in a place like this. The air was so dry that there was no smell emanating from the carcass, just the aroma of the bleached grass that looked like it hadn't seen rain in decades.

Spaces that become poetic can evolve slowly, through gentle weathering and erosion, but also through fast-striking disasters, as could be seen in a drowned place like Bombay Beach, on the eastern shore of the Salton Sea, the product of a severe ecological disaster. Located east of Los Angeles in a very arid region, the Salton Sea was created in the beginning of the twentieth century accidentally through the improper irrigation management of the Colorado River. The large, unnatural body of water was a tourist resort for a while, but subsequent increases in salinity made the area fairly uninhabitable, causing fish-kills that ultimately lead to beaches colored white because of the thorough coverage of fish bones. In Bombay Beach, the evidence of flooding is still visible, with the fringes of the impoverished settlement displaying signs of collapsed houses, flattened doors, the corroded shells of ancient automobiles, and even a relic of a doghouse with a curious lunar crescent carved into the side. During the hot summer when I visited, the air was thick with the smell of saline and rotting tilapia that wash up onto the beaches every day.

The objects and places presented here are intended as a tantalizingly brief survey across a large swath of terrain which in no way is intended as a thorough categorization or analysis; in fact, this exploration of poetic spaces in California embodies only one particularly tiny corner of the world and is but a "drop in the bucket," intended to entice those with adventurous and inquisitive dispositions to poetically investigate their own immediate surroundings. It is through this kind of exploration that poetic knowledge intersects with historical knowledge, resulting in their subsequent, transmutative interactions.

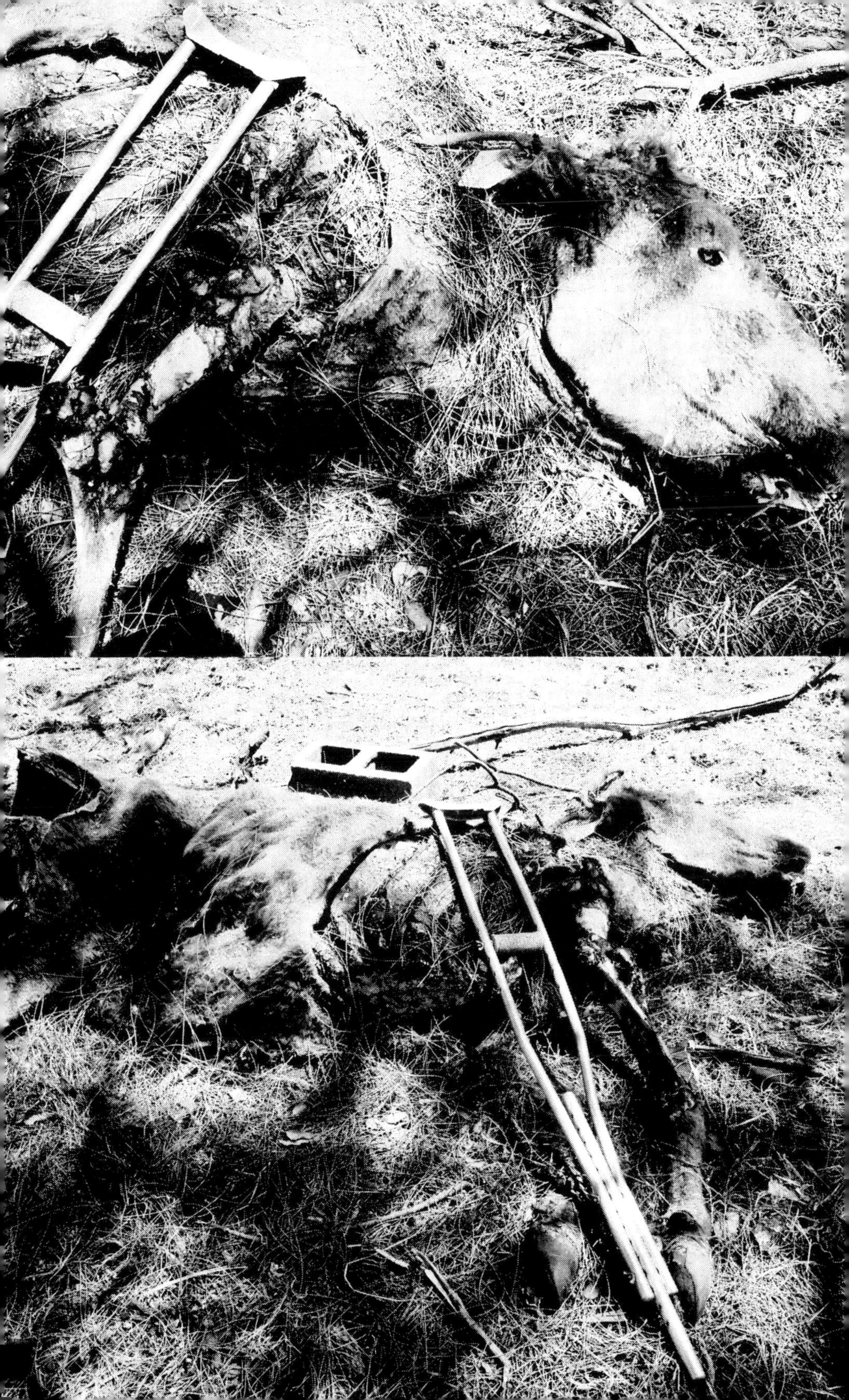

We Desire to Desire
(Communication about a magnetic surfacing in Fuencarral street)

by Ángel Zapata

We do not desire something. We desire to desire.
– Gilles Deleuze

On Saturday the 21st of July, in the afternoon, I leave home with my companion. We go to the shops in the Chueca district and from there to Fuencarral street in search of a suitable gift for friends. The street at this hour is full of people, and it is difficult to proceed through the crowd that moves in an almost ritual way from one store to the other, sometimes crossing the sidewalk or gathering in front of the shop windows.

Suddenly a small crowd on the sidewalk we are travelling makes us slow down.

Here also is a group of people that has stopped to look (and we stop with them), but the difference is that this random group isn't looking at anything, or more exactly, they are staring with fascination at nothing.

Actually, what appears before our eyes is the site of a demolished building; what is visible to us is just a hole in which there really *isn't anything to see* except for the void itself.

What could keep us in front of such a vacant lot? What is it that puzzles us? What is it that calls our attention there?

Both my companion and I remain fascinated, not so much by the hole itself, but rather by that involuntary pause, by that subtly disruptive, deeply inexplicable sensation. In fact we take a moment to assure ourselves that the group of "spectators" is being continuously renewed. And a few days later we return to the same part of the street to verify that the hole is still exerting the same attraction, a similar irresistible disturbance in the stream of passers-by.

•

By itself the second visit makes it clear that the memory of this insignificant event – nonetheless marked with strangeness – has already transformed into an insistence within me, into an enigma. I am attracted of course to the slightly oneiric quality of the scene from a few days ago which we were momentarily a part of, and also what the scene involves by way of slight distortion: of *deviation* from the increasingly repressive regime of normality.

Also, it is clear to me that the "solution" to the enigma – if there were one – would hardly be found in the realm of knowledge.

But even so, the image of that spontaneous crowd on the edge of nothingness doesn't cease to awaken all kinds of ideas and associations within me.

In line with this, it is a well known fact that within the lacanian milieu, the intervention carried out by the analyst is called "punctuation." Opposed to the tedious classical "interpretation" – that aims at *naming the meaning* of what has been stated by the patient – punctuation is often reduced by the analyst to a cut, a break, to a word that is returned emphasized with a distinct intonation or converted into a question. Punctuation, in short, aims at upsetting the complete reasoning in which the "I" unceasingly fabulates its history, at blocking that supposed "history" of the I, at replacing the reasoning *that is* the I into a question.

The capitalist city is a vast apparatus of domination and is also, by the same token, a discourse...

And in such a discourse it wouldn't be an exaggeration to affirm that today Fuencarral street is a diatribe.

In its narrow, sinuous layout, the intrusive, menacing and everpresent screaming of authoritarian merchandise is simply stunning. Just as it happens within the city itself, also here the entire area has been converted into a market. The commercial centers, the franchises connected with multinational chains have remarkably disfigured its well-known character: the saturation of life, intensity and time that this urban life had in other eras. One could say that the street itself, for all intents and purposes, has disappeared *as such*, having turned invisible, having exploded into a meaningless diaspora of fragments in the somnambulistic stretches (and therefore *full* of compulsion, of urgency, and the fear of emptiness) that here and there separate one shop window from the other, from one purchase to the next.

For capitalism, the street is the inane space that passes between two shops, or between two purchases. Life itself is nothing but "dead time," demolished and empty: the interval that unites and separates all the (supposedly significant) acts connected with the chain of production and consumption... And in this sense, it is much more than a metaphor to say that the demolished, missing building, the empty lot in Fuencarral street, really functions as an act of *punctuation* carried out within the discourse of merchandise, which is the capitalist city interpreting itself, punctuating itself, and it is within the gaps or vacant lots that its subconscious surfaces, its unstated truth which is none other than the pure reality of devastation: its *unbearability* that is fascinating, to a certain extent.

In one way then, the vacant lot is the unforeseen spectacle of nothingness presenting as evidence the nothingness of the Spectacle. A sudden "nothing-to-see" to which the capitalist subject still clings for a few moments from his daily "check-out-the goods" training; i.e., looking at the fetish that transforms him into a projection screen for nothingness: "to look-at-nothingness"...

And on the other hand, what doubt arises from the fact that the sudden appearance of the vacant lot induces an unevenness in the experience, a release, an abrupt change of register that makes the transition from the phallic jouissance – a jouissance of the "masculine" position typical of all practices connected with consumption: (the jouissance of "having," which is situated outside the body) – to the other- jouissance or "jouissance -without-object" synonymous with the feminine position and which is to be found in tight correspondence with the real body.

•

Moreover, I don't lose sight of the possibility that this interpretation perhaps falls too close to the realm of alienation (narrowly corresponding to a semiotic conception of the unconscious), and still remains outside of the *excessive nucleus* that the experience itself conveyed for me then, i.e. its specifically *poetic* dimension.

Indeed, from a strictly semiotic consideration of the unconscious, I have until now been able to maintain a diffuse synonymy – restricted to its functional value – between synonyms like "space," "hole" or "void"...

And furthermore, it becomes impossible to ignore that every genuinely surrealist experience of the unconscious leans, by its very nature, toward the intense "semantism" to which Gilbert Durand was relating, or similarly, toward the search for creative, revolutionary, poetic subjectivity, from the effectiveness not only of the chains of symbols linked together by diverse relationships, but also of the vast symbolic constellations that postulate the imbrication of everything with everything at every moment.

For the same reason, it is time to mention that the experience itself to which I am referring in this article – the poetry of this irregular, useless, and anomalous gap within the flow of an urban mobility increasingly monitored by the apparatus of capitalist Biopower – wouldn't affirm the sudden occurrence of any hypothetical "fascination of emptiness" (the favourite theme of the innumerable fire-fighters and pyromaniacs of contemporary nihilism) as much as it would affirm the random and disturbing surfacing (over the course of devastated daily life) of a living symbol deeply anchored in the unconscious and therefore highly charged: the symbol of the hole.

And indeed: both in the heritage of the mythologies and in the hermetic tradition, the hole is above all the symbol of the opening to the unknown. It is what ends up "on the other side" (exteriority in relation to the tangible), or that which ends up in the hidden (exteriority in relation to the visible). In its pictorial dimension, the hole has a richer significance than mere emptiness: in it resonate all possibilities of what could fill it, therefore alluding both to hope and to the imminence of what could come. The source of all possibilities is thus created, which therefore connects both with the symbols of fertility in the biological field, and with the doorway to the spiritual life on the mental plane.

For certain traditional cultures, the hole is an image of the female organ – the way of being born into the world, as well as a worldly gate though which death, understood as transformation, would allow one to escape from the laws of this plane of existence. As Chevalier and Gheerbrant assert in their *Dictionary of Symbols*: "therefore the hole has a double meaning, immanentist-transcendentalist: it opens the interior to the exterior, and the exterior to the Other."

The hole is thus the symbol of the absolute *outside*.

Its pregnancy is linked to the fascination of exteriority and of the future.

Its poetry is that of a sudden rip in the fabric of the given, so as to dazzle us with the light of that which will be.

•

All in all, if the semiotic consideration of the unconscious often appears short-sighted when compared with the fecundity of the specifically imaginal experience, the latter – thoroughly investigated by the hermeneutics of post-jungian orientation – runs the risk in turn of letting itself get dragged towards cheap proliferation, towards an inflated fetishizing of that meaning.

Both currents, on the other hand, develop their activity on a horizon of understanding that is dominated by healthcare – by the theorization of the human as care-of-the-self – while any approach to the unconscious that pursues a dialogue with the fertile tradition of surrealism calls for a dialectical conception of human reality and subsequently, for a consideration of the inseparable subject of revolutionary praxis.

We do not need more *meaning;* we need "more reality"...

But precisely that plus-reality cannot occur within us except as the result of a *subtraction:* as a sudden nakedness, as an abrupt lowering of all façades, of all constructions, of all appearances.

To this is directed, after all, the value of criticism, of *punctuation* and of questioning from which derives the intense magnetism of the vacant lot, its power of poetic impregnation and disturbance.

To all (the Imaginary) of desire – that enrages the Empire of the commodity by way of decoy – live chance in the street and the bright air of the city are opposed by the gap, the hole, the decline in the continuity of meaning: an emptiness in which desire and its truth surface from somewhere else.

Desire is *not* the desire for objects but the desire for desire. Desire is utopia in action.

We do not desire *something*.

We desire to desire.

The Magnetized Land

by Noé Ortega Quijano

The poetic experience of the outdoors is extremely intense because of the ability that some places have to surprise us, to undermine our ability to understand, and to submerge us in their aura from which we always emerge as changed people. Such is the case whenever we suddenly and unexpectedly encounter the *brute force of the marvellous* within those places, wide open in front of us. The intensity with which we are possessed by its open mystery varies according to countless circumstances, which turns the experience of exteriority into a particular and unique fact. These places have the ability to enrich our experience of the real, vigorously generating a charge of desire that will later be projected onto daily life. For that reason, today maybe more than ever, the search for the open and free, unexploited landscapes is necessary, since we are talking about places in which the most direct and naked experience of the real is still possible, before being articulated through any kind of conscious assimilation.

Canales is a tiny village in a rural area of Cantabria (*) that I have been connected with since childhood. So my discovery of that place occurred where the division between rationality and irrationality, pleasure and reality, dream and watchfulness did not have much influence upon my knowledge of the world. One of the features of that area which still continues to captivate me with so much intensity is the abundance of ruined buildings there. For many of them only the outer walls remain standing, while their interiors have been invaded by weeds and serve as a refuge for rodents and birds. The passage between these buildings does not fail to produce a weird shiver that seems to come from the empty recesses of their walls. Outside the village, on the hill, many other edifices are found, completely swallowed by vegetation. They are part of the infrastructure that supported the mining activity of this area that has been abandoned for many years.

It is still possible to follow a path between most of these buildings that runs through hazel-shrubs and blackberry bushes. As one proceeds towards the hill, the wooden boards and irons that formed the rails (which carried the small wagons transporting the minerals) appear on the ground. At a certain point, when the side vegetation overwhelms the road, one reaches a passage or small tunnel that was dug through the naked rock. Its mouth is pitch black due to the fact that the tunnel follows a curved course that obscures the light at the other end. In the entrance the air turns cold and humid. Proceeding into the humidity, one is immediately submerged in total darkness. It is impossible to see either the entrance or the exit. This moment is all about total isolation and vital suspension. Around here, the unknown *breathes*. One finds oneself mentally naked, defenseless and mute. One's body feels differently, and the sense of balance suffers a moment of confusion. That act of penetrating the open emptiness of the rock, of entering a total darkness in which there is a momentary doubt about whether there is an exit, constitutes for me the core of my relationship with exteriority. That tunnel is the center of gravity that binds me to that which is most profound and inexpressible on earth. Behind that *suspension of reality,* and from a few steps forward, the light of the exit can finally be glimpsed. At the end, with the darkness still overhead, a valley comes into view. It is absolutely uninhabited, and the silence that reigns is powerful. That silence, preceded by the initial passage through the obscurity of the tunnel, is imposing, and leads to a state of sensory exaltation before the magnitude of the real in this lost valley where the feeling of isolation with regards to the rest of the world is of intoxicating potency.

Having lived that experience, I can affirm, not without a certain amount of stammering, that darkness and silence, in general and as they cover that valley especially, act as catalysts of poetic materialism. However, it does not become any easier to nourish the powers of the spirit upon using the outdoors as a point of departure: now that life is to be found concentrated within cities, it is a established fact that the outdoors has almost totally ceased to be considered a natural environment where the uninhibited discovery and experience of the world can happen, to be considered in relation to the city as a counter-point. Thus the experience of exteriority is limited by the scope of culture, and furthermore remains physically delimited by the boundary where the cities end (and not just the cities, but all the lands committed one way or another to the production of goods to feed the machinery of the

commercialized city).

Darkness does not exist in the city. Electric lighting is in charge of keeping the streets lit until dawn – that time of day essential for minimizing the cost of abolishing the darkness. Paradoxically, these sources of artificial lightning, so different from the flame of the devices that preceded them, use their orange glare to hide what constitutes the only luminous source outside at night except for the moon: the stars. Indeed the already official "light pollution" *banishes* both darkness and starlight. A double cancellation thus occurs for the possibility of the poetic experience in all its amplitude. Darkness is the privileged habitat of the poetic. Where the occult forces unfold, where one shakes before the unknown, where the unguarded act, the escape and the conspiracy all take place, where the liberation of desire and the transgression of norms are possible, where the moon rises, moving the oceans, and the creatures venture out to wander the woods: that is the territory of poetry. It is still possible to find favorable places in the city, but only to the extent that a certain type of shadow is often found there, existing as only a diluted form of darkness manifested in the urban environment.

The position of the heavenly bodies, and especially of the North Star, constitutes one of the means of orientation based on the observation of nature. There is only one ship more beautiful than the shipwreck: the phosphorescent one that navigates under the North Star while the other stars spin in a sky of panther fur. Of all the human abilities, the capacity of global orientation is one that implies an intimate relationship of man with the world. It results from needing to know the terrain and location, and relies directly on the observable experience of physical reality: the observation of moss growing on the northern face of tree bark or of the position of the rise and fall of the solar disk are part of a scheme that is inseparable from the world. It is precisely the contrary that happens with orientation methods that are imposed today, where the global positioning system (GPS) and digital maps disconnect people from the world with mathematical precision. The most serious problem with this disconnection is that not only does a separation occur (in and of itself dramatic), but further still, that all possibilities of getting lost disappear. The hegemony of the virtual world, from the digitalized representation of the terrain and its display on a computer screen deny the existence of unknown places in favor of a system that only requires data on the coordinates, distances, addresses or elevation. This entire set of pseudoinformation displaces manifest knowledge and negates the entity of spaces as such, substituting them interminably with the means *to get somewhere else*. The situation worsens in the city where everything is labelled with signs, where evacuation routes are thoroughly predetermined, where all cardinal references external to the city itself lack any importance (beyond the taxable value of the buildings' orientation) and where, in the end, the necessity of *independently* orienting oneself has vanished.

But aside from these issues we should not forget that the *disconnection* primarily occurs at a much more basic level, by means of the asphalt and pavement which separate us from the natural soil and its incessant pulse. This pulse, from which we are deprived of direct contact in the city, is especially intense in the definitive nerve centers of the outdoors. "Las Arenas Rojas" [Red Sands] is the name of an area situated on the slope of a hill near Canales. It is nothing more than a dumping-ground surrounded by thorn-bushes and nettles. The fact that the whole hill is covered with vegetation except for that bare area could almost make one consider this sandy ground as a sore rising from the mantle of the earth. There was such an abundance of minerals that when we were kids, we rushed there in a state of great excitement, and each time someone found a mineral that was especially fantastic, we gathered around it, fascinated by the magic of the ancient crystals. But the peculiar impact of that place is due to much more profound forces than the mere play of light from the crystals. The name of the place comes from the reddish colour of the ground caused by the high density of hematites in the area. Far beyond the magic of the shining surfaces of these stones, its potency is rooted in its magnetic activity: on this slope earthly magnetism is being altered – to whatever extent – by a ground seeded with magnets. Maybe it is the presence of the hematites and their hypothetical magnetic influences that explain Arenas Rojas' strange power of seduction. It is interesting to know that the name of the mineral comes from the Greek word to denote blood: the ground here is impregnated with the blood of the earth. Open in its living flesh, pulsating, the magnetized earth whispers seductively to summon and retain the affective disposition of whoever sets foot on that wound.

There is another fact that imbues the soil of that area with richness. It has to do with the abundance of chasms and hidden caves in the limestone rock, which reaffirms the almost tangible presence of the unknown. Some of these caves are similar to nearby Altamira, where the bison within its uterus of stone were tatooed precisely with hematite dust of iron oxides. If one climbs the slope of the red sands and follows a path that borders the valley from the top of the hill, one can reach Cueva de las Cáscaras [Shell Cave], so named because of the disquieting presence of numerous shell deposits, the only remaining trace of the ancient sea that once covered these lands. There are many more caves scattered throughout the hills, and for the most part, they are unknown. One of them is found at the bottom of a chasm at about thirty meters deep, to which one can gain access through the underbrush at one of its entrances. Eagles hide their nests on the vertical walls of the chasm. The mouth of the cave is not visible until one practically stands right next to it. The descent into the bowels of the rock is overwhelming. Once you are a few meters inside, the stalactites and the incessant dripping initiate an immersion into an unknown dominion of time.

I have already mentioned the state of abandon of the mine infrastructure in the area, which caused the mountains, apart from the caves, to be riddled with empty tunnels and wells. The center of the valley is the enclave where Hoyo del Pilugo [Pilugo Hole] is located, the vertical, now sealed entrance to one of the tunnels. In another part of the valley, on the slope where the curved tunnel can be found, is Pozo de Peñamontero [a mine shaft], another one of the many points of access to the mines. Even though the small buildings situated in the surroundings are totally ruined, the shaft is still preserved in a fairly good state. Here one can see remains of the elevator machinery. But now the shaft that was once occupied by the elevator is empty. I have visited this place for years, and I still stick to the tradition from my childhood where we would drop a stone through the dark hole, letting our gaze penetrate the blackness, trying to follow its descent, and for a period of time that seemed endless, we continued to listen until the echo of the stone reached our ears. I lack the words to explain how the fall of the stone drags the mind in with it and how, during that moment of silence while the stone is falling (plunging into the darkness, lost from sight and accelerating in its fall), the sensation of groundlessness penetrates the chest, is felt in the blood and sends

the mind into upheaval. Only the echo allows life to resume, already irreversibly affected by the deep. I consider that act as being an essential, intrinsic part of what constitutes the surrealist experience of exteriority. And I do so maybe without being fully aware of it, without being able to articulate this experience, but this is how it is whenever the experience happens with a blinding power released at full-force, with an almost elemental and primal nakedness.

The night of lightning has crossed these regions on innumerable occasions. In the city, the power of the storm is neutralized when the lightning rods have stopped their destructive potential. But here the arrival of the storm makes even the core of the rock shiver. I have witnessed storms of frightening violence. In several occasions dead cattle have been found, and roofs and walls destroyed. In the last century, the stable of the house where I live now burned down one night following the impact of a bolt. A few years ago, during a night of strong wind from the northwest, lightning struck our house quite near the refrigerator that was standing close to us. For a fraction of a second reality burst wide open. The electric whip left the air suspended in an unbearable, ionized silence. That sensation of vulnerability, of finding oneself in front of a an uncontrollable and unknown reality of colossal proportions fertilizes the relationship between the mind and the world and makes it appear to us in all its depth, so far-removed from the superficial, decorative and inoffensive aspect that the society of well-being tries to sell us.

In these places, in this magnetized earth and in this ionized air, time flows free, radically remote from the dominant, vital rhythm of the cities where it comes marked from outside according to necessities that are not ours. The world moves along, outside the laws of urban life in addition to its logic of meetings, chance events and discoveries. Life accommodates itself to the pulse of the earth and the position of the sun, to the obscurity of the tunnels and to the uninhabited valley, remaining fortified by the power of the physicality of those certain places where mystery attracts. Except for the local character marked by one's own experience, I think that many of the essential features of experiencing the outdoors are similar and to be found planted within these moments of vital suspension.

The last time I entered the Cueva de las Cáscaras, it was around mid-day, at the time of the highest elevation of the sun. After having passed the red sands I went into the hill and there found something amazing. It is no less significant that this has been the only discovery, in the most concrete and tangible sense, that I have witnessed in a region where searching and discovering do not exist separately as such, but rather occur simultaneously in the experience of the outdoors. It was the mouth of a drain-pipe, totally out of place and whose presence there I still cannot explain to myself, on top of which was the hoof of a deer cut off by some predator. The articulation of the extremity was situated in the center of the pipe, of a form totally analogous to the clock-hands in the middle of an unusual sphere. Hours of hunting and nettles, of caves and lightning bolts.

On this magnetized earth swing the shining needles of time.

(*) on the northern coast of Spain. Translator's note.

Beyond the Walls of the City

by Julio Monteverde

I. The perception of the city limits

Who hasn't felt the urge, while travelling, to walk into the woods that flank the road, to open the door of your running car and to disappear among the pines and the cypresses? It is a childish desire kindled in the minds of travellers: the unknown that reveals itself to us. Or what is worse, the intuition of this unknown immensity that surrounds a well-travelled, two-way road. It would be so simple to step out and disappear in the woods… Somebody must have done it. Somebody freer, more disposed to enter what is there but which is unknown.

When I was a child, living in a provincial city, the quiet edge of the city could be seen through the window of the living room. I write that it could be seen, but I quickly understand that this expression doesn't do justice to the power of that experience. In the afternoon, in the overwhelming silence at half past four, the edge of the city was felt like a sleeping beast. Its presence seemed to invade the houses, transforming the appearance of everything in our neighborhood. In those days the city limits could be mentally traced with a line that coincided with a railroad that has now become invisible. That boundary was continuously being pushed inwards by the presence of the outskirts on the horizon. The city outskirts, during certain hours of the day, completely threw us for a loop.

The contact with those limits may very well be the one that influenced me the most, and which had a strange persistence in the emotion I felt each time I contemplated, in any issue of the children's magazine *Mortadelo y Filemón*, the latest comics depicting the characters hiding from certain punishment in the outskirts of the city and, above all, with what I came to identify for the first time as a truly open field. Such a presence seemed to mean a journey and it revealed to me the possibility of leaving the city by my own means. My daydreaming led me to imagine myself (who, like any other kid, had *also* been educated in the fear of becoming a *lost child*) arriving naturally in these fortuitously remote places, without interruption, *since there was nothing to stand in my way.*

II. The absent walls

The ancient walls of the city served as protection against the outside. In times of war, as in times of peace, its main function was to control the traffic. Yet not all urban settlements had walls, and many of them were demolished when the needs of the town required it, for example when over-crowding became unbearable. The walls, that safeguarded economic activity and the security of property, never posed a threat to the real mobility of the inhabitants who could easily live away from them and enter their perimeter to make commercial transactions, or when a dangerous situation made it necessary. In this way, anybody who wanted to enter or leave the city unavoidably had to do so through designated passages that closed at sunset. But their function ended there. Their presence was obvious and practically insurmountable, but their power was concentrated and concrete.

If a regular army tried to enter one of our large western cities today, it would first need to traverse an exasperating maze of suburbs and false cities, all in vain. Not to mention that the possibility of establishing an old-fashioned siege would be ridiculous. The interconnections of all kinds of pathways, ghostly suburbs, car dealerships, golf courses and gas stations have expanded so much that the city has totally lost its limits, and what is part or not part of the urban center can only be determined through intuition. The walls, the old walls have disappeared from the urban horizon. Nevertheless: can we enter or leave the city *freely and by our own means?*

It would be very interesting to organize an expedition from the center of a city with the intention of leaving it on foot in order to reach the point that doubtlessly could be considered an open space. An exterior where we really could feel the air of the outdoors on our faces. Lamentably, this expedition would be doomed to become a dull trek, and doubtlessly the fatal boredom that the quite restless and adventure-craving explorer would experience would soon endanger him. Sooner or later he would have to deal with the journey's impossibility, its boredom, or a lack of time to complete it.

There is an essential difference on this point regarding the old urban dwellings and the new ones. The ways in and out have always been controlled. Nowadays, however, these paths have vanished in such a way that they truly prevent a thorough exit from them. One can leave the *urban center* (understood as *polis* [or city-state]), but leaving the *"urban"* (understood as the capitalist system which produces relations that are unique to it, as a place for the establishment and development of a calculating economy) is practically impossible. Wherever we go – and we know this very well – we find the colonization of capital: that colonization simply known either as tourism (1), or as a liquidation of the *Experience of the Outside* and the subsequent replacement of its likeness to be put up for sale. The highways, the very means of transportation in and of themselves, are also part of the city, taken as the residential domain of capital – extensions of a center that isn't just the city but capitalism itself. If the existence of the city has left its original center so as to adapt itself to the priorities of the economy, and if the life that was its driving force (cafés, theaters, cinemas as places of social meeting that shaped the soul of the city through the daily relationships of its inhabitants) has been substituted by what has now really become the center of common life, where its true nature currently resides (banks, real-estate agencies, department stores, fast food restaurants that promote frantic circulation and prevent a more substantial existence) (2), this relocation [of capital] has not, despite the process of urban centralization, lead to the liberation of those peripheral areas outside of the city that are considered marginal. No, that would be too easy. The truth is that the economy has advanced evenly so as to reach even the most remote areas. However, that extension has not occurred overnight. In fact capitalism has not eliminated those open spaces that are external to its relations (it would be physically impossible, obviously). What it has done instead is to hinder the movements and the destinations of those who are inside of it, to the point where it becomes very difficult for them to escape, or for them to find those places that don't have a price-tag. It has made them practically unreachable. The invention of the car has obviously been crucial, and the network of highways implies a progressive disappearance of the old roads and their travellers – perhaps not in any intentional way, since capitalism remains indifferent to the remnants of antiquity, but a disappearance, nevertheless (3). The alternatives have become heroic ones (4), i.e. they have ceased to be viable alternatives and have become outlets reserved for a few stubborn people who, in order to give free rein to their necessity for fresh air, need to make excessive efforts (without mentioning the obligatory payment, for lack of anything better), in order to fuel this longing for escape from everything offered one way or another by the economy. And this occurs to the extent that the edge of the city and open countryside appear to have been erased from human experience and no longer have a natural place in the imagination. The open field has thus been eliminated from the minds of the city-dwellers who can no longer think of it in a free way or even relate to it (5). We know that the human imagination is incapable of creating anything. However it has an extraordinary, almost endless ability to combine already existing elements. The less someone knows, the less possibilities he will have to create new scenarios based on his previous knowledge of disparate realities. The open field has therefore been eliminated from consciousness to the extent that the old points of reference that once made it so well-known have disappeared or have become truly extraordinary, leaving in their place a void that prevents the understanding of that existence. Outside the city, of capital, there is already nothing. Communication has been interrupted, and the open field is shrinking more and more to the point of becoming totally invisible. Once we reach that point, its extinction becomes imminent, since what can no longer be contemplated can no longer remain comprehensible, other than in an abstract way – in the same way that the concepts of death or nothingness "exist." What remains thereafter are only the televized nature documentaries that bring all of the exotic and thereby unreachable into our homes. In the meantime the exterior that surrounds us doesn't and will never again exist.

However, that impossibility has its price. In fact, everything that happens to humanity has its price.

III. The impossible odyssey

There will always be a movement of reaction against coercion. Directed, for better or for worse, the response always arrives and is dependent on the means of articulation possessed by the individual who confronts what has provoked him or who instead takes flight in whatever direction. Most of the time, for better or for worse, everything ends up getting sublimated. Without a doubt, modern cinema represents the best means of sublimating the impulses and fears of humanity within capitalist society, and the spirit of this era can be found in it without needing to search very hard and without the fear of being mistaken. It is no secret that the extension of capitalism and the actual impossibility of escaping it provoke a claustrophobic sensation, if not in manifest form – the major part of the individuals in these societies have grown within it and do not know anything else – then otherwise as an intuition that indefinitely whispers its longing for freedom. In today's prevalent conditions of daily life, there is a core of emptiness provoked by the impossibility of finding other opportunities, of being able to rely on them in order to create one's own life. We're talking about a wretched mutilation of the possibilities that man depends on within his imagination to establish the base of his existence. And this amputation that has occurred, as we have said, through the progressive elimination of the ability to imagine oneself anywhere outside the capitalist experience centered in technological comfort, has left the hint of increasing dissatisfaction deep within the minds of people. That doesn't mean that the individual understands his or her situation in an exact and immediate way, but this is the case when confronted by a narrative in which his or her difficulties are being expressed symbolically, upsetting the individual with the intuition that this story in one way or another articulates his or her unconscious thought. This quality, so characteristic of myths, is clearly noticed within a handful of movies nearly all made and shown symptomatically during the last two or three years of the 20th century, which transpose that necessity, taking part one way or another in the fantastic, the last refuge of consciousness when it is allowed to escape a censorship that maintains an iron grip on its real experience through *the symbolic*. The problem with the fantastic on this point is that the process of interpretation is often impeded by the manifest plot itself, which is never sufficient, and never reaches the desired level of *comprehension*, or its desired trajectory, to put it simply. Such is the case in some of these movies. However, the degree to which these symbols are interiorized, when considered in and of themselves, can sometimes happen to be so profound that they provoke within the viewer an unaffected tendency towards a typical response. When the

spectator, according to the conditions of his or her own life, encounters difficulties analogous to the ones already seen within the symbolic state of the narrative, this person will articulate a response, thinking that in reality it is he or she who has provoked it, without knowing exactly where these impulses came from, but having the assurance that they already existed before manifesting themselves. And this person will be correct. In the field of popular culture – and despite its perpetual *uniqueness* – only cinema is likely to offer these narratives nowadays (6).

Everything begins, as we have said, with intuition, with a void that seems to grow within the human being and through which the experience starts to change into a sinister masquerade. This emptiness is detectable from various shortcomings that make us suspect that something much bigger and darker is in fact hiding behind the impossibility of escape. In the film *Dark City* we bear witness to a disclosure of this type. Due to an unexpected accident, the protagonist finds himself suddenly outside of the soporific system that propagates mundane life. This disruption facilitates the questioning of his experience. Everything seems to indicate that the answers to his questions will be found *outside*. But his efforts to leave the city that imprisons him are in vain. When he takes a taxi with the intent of going to the place outside of the city where he hopes to find answers to his questions, the driver suddenly forgets the way out. It was there, in his memory, but suddenly it is rendered impossible: he has forgotten the way. The following attempt to leave the city is by subway. Nothing easier than waiting for the train that will bring him to the end of the line. But the train that would take him there doesn't stop; it just invariably passes through the station. Something similar occurs to the main character of *The Truman Show*: nothing easier than taking a means of transportation to get him out of the city where he has spent all his life. However, something happens every time he tries. Flights are delayed for months, and buses suffer irreparable breakdowns as soon all the passengers have taken their seats. In the meantime, countless messages advise him to accept his destiny of becoming a caged animal (7).

That sensation is taken one step further in the movie, *The Thirteenth Floor*. In an atmosphere of travels through time and virtual realities, the protagonist receives the order to leave the city following a route that he has never taken, to drive his car with the only objective of leaving through ways off the beaten path. He will even have to break the barriers that indicate where the roads end. At a given moment, he will identify what he feared. Unexpectedly, reality – his reality – ends. There is nothing more beyond it. It isn't that he can't continue driving, but rather that reality doesn't exist only a couple of steps ahead of him. The exterior has been eliminated as unnecessary for the control of the center.

The necessity of control that is being addressed in all these movies reaches its utmost intensity in *The Village*. Despite the fact that the symbol of confinement is present on various levels (of which some are more complex than others), it is clear that the situation of the characters in their bizarre imprisonment within the limits of a forest clearing is imposed by a conscious decision based on certain dire circumstances that form part of a great deception to which the individuals are submitted. The fact that it is done "for their own good" doesn't soften this harsh cruelty.

Yet it is in the previously mentioned movie, *The Truman Show*, where the entirety of this impossible odyssey finds its most beautiful and clarifying attention. As we have said about the movie *The Village*, *The Truman show* also functions on different levels, all of utmost interest (televized life, social relationships defined by custom and driven by necessity, the construction of a protective and empty world that is offered as an ideal but all of whose characteristics nevertheless are adapted to the needs of surveillance and control), but in particular, when considering the struggle of the human being who flees the confines of a world emptied by capitalism with the purpose of finding his own life outside of that very same world, this movie seems to have devoted its energies towards offering an impeccable narrative. The struggle of Truman (who is a romantic hero adapted to modern circumstances – as if people haven't figured that out by now)(8), is the struggle to get out, to find one's own way to the outside, a path that is understood as doubtlessly one's own, and which should confront that entire system designed to keep him inside, whether he likes it or not. And the good thing about *The Truman Show* as a story is that it doesn't fall for the temptation of trying to explain the claustrophobia in terms of a fantastic and more-or-less transcendent scenario, but instead remains linked explicitly to the conditions in which the capitalist individual conducts his life. Herein resides its greatness – a greatness that hasn't been equally perceived by everyone and regarding which it certainly remains almost impossible to judge the degree of consciousness of its creators, but that maybe precisely for that reason turns it into a time-bomb for so many minds who feel, just like Truman does (and we do too), that very same sense of impossibility, and the anxiety to get out.

IV. Last bow and exit

The need to leave and to connect, even if sporadically and only as a mere probability, exists within people as an integral, referential part of their imagination. But what happens when the need to escape remains, even when the outer fringes of the mental horizon are eliminated? All of these movies deal with that impossibility. However, for my part I think the scene that most dramatically reveals the emptiness of the imagination where man suffers within capitalist society, as I already commented, is the one in *The Thirteenth Floor*, where the main character reaches the limit of reality to find that there is nothing on the other side. Because of and beyond the fact that those areas which don't truly pertain to the economy have been neglected, the problem seems to extend to these places, according the logic of capitalism *avant la lettre*, and subsequently they cease to have their own existence, becoming more and more trivial until finally disappearing from the imagination and becoming impossible to conceptualize in their real existence. Thus everything leads us to think that *they cannot exist*. Something will occur, at the last moment, which prevents us from reaching them, and that final impossibility will achieve a brilliant cohesion within the individual's imagination. There is the suspicion, already planted firmly in the contemporary unconscious, that *one cannot leave*.

Such is the state of colonization that has been established in our lives, and such is the magnitude of that micropower of which Foucault spoke, which ultimately seeks to control the smallest physical movement of the human body so as to put it, like it or not, into the sphere of total commercialism, starting with the means of communication and relation, and ending with the vital space itself where the body of the individual moves daily (9).

Under these circumstances the destruction of imagination has no way to be stopped. It is a monotonous and constant labor that aims to focus everyone's attention on the commercialistic process of whatever is at hand. Everything else *will fall by its own weight.* The exterior, just like the future, can be considered only as an extension of what exists, and all *other* possibilities will encounter severe obstacles when entering the imagination, lacking a place to settle and anchor themselves, with the result that their movement could only be understood as a perpetual stroll within the Moebius strip of capitalism, or a never-ending recuperation of the same state of things.

The repopulation of human imagination is a task that can no longer wait. From the furthest reaches of the desert spread the rumors of refusal. Where are those spaces to be found which don't belong to anyone? Where are the places in which our relationship with them will have no other aim than that of the awakening? The utopia of presence, like a handful of seeds. The possibility of drawing new maps on which are found the best spots for the multiplication of desire. But without a point of support outside the economy, it is impossible to get it overturned. Or similarly: without a part of our thought projected into the future, it is impossible to leave the continuous present. The day will come when all of us, like Truman, will end this great comedy and, upon making a theatrical bow to the audience, we will leave *that* reality in order to find what relates to our own lives outside of it.

The Thirteenth Floor (Josef Rusnak, 1999)
Dark City (Alex Proyas, 1998)
The Village (M. Night Shyamalan, 2004)
The Truman Show (Peter Weir, 1998)
The Matrix (Larry & Andy Wachowski, 1999)

1. One could think, during a journey, that one's mental disposition would protect him from the absurdities of the tourist's view of existence. However, at least when interacting with his surroundings, one will understand very quickly that, except for how one looks on the outside, there is no qualitative difference between himself and, for example, a group of Japanese. And that's what it's all about.
2. See Ignacio Castro: *Mutations of the decentered city* in the magazine *Salamandra* #13/14, 2003-04.
3. The carts drawn by animals could take to the highway but it is quite certain that their drivers would avoid doing so at all costs. Not to mention the cyclists who are practically compelled to choose suicide when taking advantage of the quality of our roads.

4. Rural tourism cannot be taken seriously as an alternative. A form of tourism in which the offered housing is conveniently replete with all manner of technological gadgets (television, hot water, microwave...). The owners of these houses are well aware of the risks that they take by not equipping them with the same comforts as the ones found in the urban areas.
5. When talking here about cities, I am mainly referring to the big ones. In the small cities there still exists a relationship with the city-limits, even if they have been totally transformed by the car, the absolute form of travel in these urban centers, including the smallest ones. Yet proximity can't prevent this separation, as such. In the coastal areas the relationship with the sea, for example, is brutally subjected to the tourist experience, the urbanization, the seafront walks and the marinas.
6. Literature and art are totally impotent on this point, already so constrained and alienated from themselves, such that any desirable effect is lost among the folds of their own self-reference, when not of their absurd persistence through and for the commercial market. Only poetry remains with its systematic power to articulate human necessities, being rooted precisely in the direct experience itself. If literature can speak of emptiness, poetry – when worthy of the name – speaks from emptiness; it is the experience itself without any mediation (except language's essential mediation, but only if considered necessary). Criticism is doubtlessly another of the great weapons available to explain the world, however, and its role is a decisive one regarding the rational and manifest aspects of the problem, while poetry and, as we said, certain narratives that share with it certain aspects of the symbolic, operate within the latent content.
7. In a certain way that sentiment is also to be found in the film *The Matrix*, symbolized in the will to "wake up" to reality. However, the value of *The Matrix*, in my view, is reduced to being a mixture of a whole series of old myths (the revolt of the machines is nothing more than the myth of the Golem readapted, having enjoyed an amazing state of growth over the past fifty years through science fiction and the comics) and of other more modern ones and some being formulated now (Debord's society of the spectacle crushed by sci-fi imagination), blended mostly with minimal discernment, all being treated negligently in a kind of mythologic syncretism. I am speaking of the original movies, of course, as their sequels are nothing but deplorable megaproductions.
8. It is enough to mention the final struggle between Truman and the elements, in which Truman binds himself to his boat during the storm and vociferously challenges the forces of nature (which in this case actually aren't anything but the maneuvers of capital as image-spectacle).
9. In the outside as well as within the most daily interior. Recently, the character in a well-known American sitcom, upon hearing that a friend was lacking TV, asked him in amazement: "And in which direction is the furniture turned in your house?"

Three Places

by Vicente Gutiérrez

1

I've always been attracted by those places halfway between nature and the city; hybrid territories where the urban experience coexists with the experience of the outdoors. This occurs—and it seems to be when their presence most effects us—when after wandering disconcertedly down unfamiliar streets—I'm thinking now of Santander—when you come upon one of those districts that are no longer clearly urban: an unexpected landscape, an enormous field or a wooded area in which without our noticing it the presence of urban elements has gradually disappeared.

Regrettably, sooner or later these areas end up being swallowed wholly or in part by urban renewal. A good example of this is found in the vicinity of what until recently was known as La Vaguada de las Llamas. It was an undeveloped gully about three kilometers long running parallel to the city of Santander. Until a short time ago it was a singular area of wetlands, marshes and reed bogs of great biological and scenic value. But in recent years it's been encroached upon by urban development. A series of recently undertaken activities with great impact has resulted in the loss of surface area and diversity in the ecosystem; metallic roadways and cement trucks have occupied the zone, which means it is no longer an open space. This deterioration has been accompanied by a huge loss of biodiversity; on the one hand the nesting areas of numerous species of birds, amphibians and mammals have been destroyed; and on the other the incursion of exotic flora has increased, and they are steadily gaining ground on native species. As a result, it's currently impossible to move freely about the area.

Throughout my life I've gone there to partake of this *experience of the open*. Maybe the experience was strangely more marked in the gully because of its proximity to the city. Its hybrid character increased over the years due to various factors: the numerous apartment buildings that began to spring up in the vicinity (on the Valdenoja side), and the uncontrolled dumping of refuse of various kinds, as well as the glutting of a large part of the greensward with debris and other waste from construction taking place at one end. All this increased the contrast between the natural and the urban, enhancing the evocative power of the former. Its presence seemed to be accompanied by a kind of howl of protest, a desperate cry for help.

I also found interesting the way in which places like this become fixed in our unconscious; it was enough to go there and look for a poetic relation to be established that days later would find its unexpected echo in a dream. Throughout 2007 I registered 17 dreams associated with the place. In this way exteriority gradually left a trace in my interior, enchanting it again, and although—or perhaps because—this territory is now destroyed, it resists disappearing, and it does so by knocking at the gates of the unconscious. Something undoubtedly throbs beneath the concrete and the mortar in those places that have been taken over by power, occasionally struggling to return. And that happens because these already vanished zones still survive as psycho-geographic territories etched with fire in our unconscious.

In a specific spot of the gully there's a tree. Some of the dreams connected to La Vaguada take place there. This spot became something like a crater left by the impact of a meteor: an energy spot. The tree is still there today, but it's bounded by a grotesque block of concrete used for the roadway and surrounded by planks that crisscross the nearby marsh. In recent walks I couldn't avoid the temptation of going there, and even of touching the tree in a moving ritual of reencounter. A few days ago I touched its branches and tried to break-off a twig, but was disagreeably surprised to find that its branches were like rubber and wouldn't break. Another example of how we internalize these kinds of natural spots is the following: in another dream I saw myself rowing a boat through the most inundated area of the reed bog, something which at first seemed absurd, because I'd never seen anyone doing that. A few days later I learned that until the beginning of the 20th century the Vaguada de las Llamas was a *ría,* (a long, narrow fjord-like inlet) that began at what today is the beach of El Sardinero, and that many people made the trip in small boats. For me it was quite significant that this fact was revealed to me in a dream.

2

Now I'll discuss places subjected to the opposite process: urban enclaves that nature has recovered and once again occupied. I've always felt particularly attracted by submerged villages. And perhaps even more forcefully, by villages that have reemerged; places that, after a long eclipse, reappear drenched in the watery flow of time. Their mere contemplation offers numerous sources of the marvelous. In 2006 I visited Lagüelles, located in the province of León. It's a village in the county of Luna, in Babia, on the right bank of the Luna River. The construction of a dam on the Luna resulted in the town's disappearance beneath the waters of the reservoir. But it isn't always submerged, sometimes it just remains isolated. When each year the level of the Luna Reservoir drops, other submerged villages emerge; they gradually become visible in this order, depending on the water level: Arévalo, Santo Olaja, Láncara, Lagüelles, Campo, Oblanca, San Pedro, Miñera, Mirantes, Ventas de Mallo and Venta de la Canela. But Lagüelles perhaps conserves the most architectural elements.

You can reach it on foot, though there's no well-marked trail for tourists. This inaccessible character attracted me even more. The climate, although somewhat cold and damp, is quite healthy. The area is extensive and well supplied with vegetation. In Lagüelles the rock walls separating properties are still visible, as well as the stone walls and wooden beams of some houses, and the odd cobbled square. Also, emblematic features such as the bell tower, the mill beside the river or the approach roads, flanked by the cadavers of upright trees. One sees, during this fading of vision, the inert presence of the people who lived here. My visit to this place caused within me an uncontrollable vertigo, accompanied by a successive loss of awareness. This happened at certain moments when I became separated from the group I was with. This is a phenomenon that anyone can easily verify for themselves, by gradually approaching any place with similar characteristics. I imagine that this state is caused by the exaggerated depth of the external, which is augmented by the fact that everything there has been inundated for long periods by hundreds of cubic meters of water. All the weight of this water that's *now gone* hangs over you. *A new order of seeing* is inaugurated in Lagüelles. Curiously, *to be in Babia*—Babia is Luna's adjoining county—is a saying that means to be absorbed in one's own thoughts, a malady of the itinerant shepherds

in the remote pastures of Extremadura. In my case, this self-absorption came from without, not from within, and it remained without, swirling around in the observed. It's what looks at itself that becomes self-absorbed as a surface. And my state was nothing but a feverish feeling of profound correspondence, a correspondence in no way reflexive. The fact that mere contemplation could isolate me from any thoughts of a reflexive or referential kind constitutes in and of itself a disconcerting *poetics of the incomprehensible.* Between this sort of fainting, and the subsequent state of recuperation, were things: the ruins, the corpses of standing trees, the soaking wet rocks flung about everywhere, the remains of facades... became transfigured into entities that were stripped of meaning, entities yet to have meaning, thus acquiring a mysterious nature. This placed them in a kind of suspension in which manifold meanings fluctuate, and that inspires a vertigo of astonishment very different than the feeling that these same objects would arouse in me in their original context. I've noticed that this phenomenon, as intense as it is and feeling like it would last forever, is followed by a swift process of recovery in which consciousness once again recognizes them for what they were, but with the difference that they have left an emotional residue in our interior. Furthermore, it was as though these new entities were about to begin moving, to disorganize themselves more than they already were, to configure improvised labyrinths where they could lose themselves time and again. In his book, *H*, Eugenio Castro mentions an emblematic place: Mt. Torcal. By virtue of its characteristics, Eugenio considers it an ideal site for giving free reign to passionate amorous energy: "In reality, certain passions have not found a more favorable setting for their unfolding, a place where they could satisfy their ineffable destiny, than in the rocky topography of certain mountains, where there, and only there, they could culminate. It's exciting to recognize in the rocks of the mountains a majestic and essential setting where lovers can liberate their passionate energy"(1). Unfortunately, I've never visited Mt. Torcal, but I have to admit that feelings very similar to those described by Eugenio overcame me in Lagüelles. Moisture for me has always had a significant association with the erotic, and I'm sure that that half-submerged village is the place where moisture has assumed a leading role. During my visit I took advantage of the occasion to collect stones. They all had one thing in common: they were soaked, and moisture was so much a part of them that they seemed to have a life of their own. I found one stone in which the action of the water and the successive changes in pressure had provoked a strange physical effect: the stone was divided into five segments about 2 centimeters thick each. The aesthetic and tactile pleasure that stone produced in me is indescribable. I discerned in it something related to the unbearable nature of amorous pleasure.

3

Finally, and in no way opposed to the above, I'd like to speak about certain other places that immerse us in a state of *absolute openness*. I'm referring to those natural settings where there is a complete lack of manmade objects or buildings.

In the summer of 2007 I visited Norway. I couldn't resist the temptation to visit the fjords. We boarded a boat in Gudvanen. I couldn't say what specific route we followed since in order to better enjoy what I was seeing, I refused to consult a map. Afterward I tried to identify the inlet we sailed up, but I'm still not sure if it was the Aurlandsfjord or the Norsyfjord . At any rate, it was one of the best boat trips I've ever taken, only comparable to a trip I made in the delta of the Danube. While the boat advanced slowly, I thought I saw in these fjords a slight opening movement, like an embrace, that was connected to the movement of the boat. The incessant opening of enormous crags functioned as external elements, remote from me, that didn't cease to unfold; toward what? The lofty waterfalls scattered about the landscape and possessing a mysterious electricity, let fall the enigma of their very presence. I've never experienced abandonment such as that. At every instant I had the feeling of being before something inexplicable, something that if in previous experiences was in itself perturbing, in this case was made even more wrenching. Nothing, not even the boat transporting me, reminded me of anything connected with civilization. I'm not sure I can describe my state; the only thing I can even attempt to say is that I was never conscious of my ego, to the point that the sudden sensation of being before an inexhaustible, incomprehensible, absolute landscape seemed more real than my own presence.

The boat trip ended in Flam, on the shore of the Aurland fjord. We stopped for coffee there and waited for the departure of Norway's most famous scenic train, the Flamsbana. In Flam I discovered that the boat ride among the fjords had lasted two hours, but such was my state of visual intoxication, that I was convinced the trip had lasted more than triple that.

Undoubtedly this great distancing from the city and its elements is essential for fully experiencing—as I did among the fjords—what we call exteriority. As I said, it's within reach of anyone.

1. Eugenio Castro, *H.* Pepitas de Calabaza, 2006. p. 129.

Finis Urbis

by José Manuel Rojo

One Sunday in January 2007 Lurdes Martinez and I together visited an exhibition dedicated to the *Movida* of Madrid organized in the old brewery El Águila, now converted (as usual and unfortunately), into a library or a cultural center whose ridiculous, populist name I don't feel like mentioning, a cosmetic operation intended to redeem the odious past of the old industries with the hue of culture, simultaneously abolishing the poetic charge of certain abandoned factories, precisely *as such*. As they are, postmodern cosmetics aren't all that thorough, since one of the attractions of the visit, given our shared interest in industrial archeology, was to get to know the superb building from the early 1900's, an interest that didn't go unfulfilled. It should be clarified that this factory is situated in the Arganzuela district, exactly at the border between two of its neighborhoods, Palos de Moguer to the north and Delicias to the south, and that Arganzuela was an industrial zone at the beginning of the 20th century, a dubious golden age from which many testimonies still remain, even if almost all of them are silent and empty ones, as the place has been gradually transformed into a large archeological deposit under the open sky, subdued as well by the speculation that the old factories and the homes of workers are to be destroyed so as to make way for luxurious residential areas. And in a way, the exhibition itself was archeological since it gathered the broken pieces, records, covers, photographs and articles of clothing from what was once a state of mind fed by emotion and energy but which today looks dissected and divided into respective "artistic disciplines" just like the pieces of amphora or mosaic from a vanished civilization and actually, like these pieces, lacking any real importance except for the utilitarian value that they once had when alive and vibrant.

After leaving the exhibit we walked up the hill of General Lacy Street under a grey winter sky without meeting anyone, a solitude that I ascribed to the fact that it was a holiday. Shortly after having started walking, I felt a strong sensation of emptiness, of solitude, doubtlessly

influenced by the atmospheric conditions and the absence of people; an inner and outer emptiness, a disturbing but not anguishing sensation like the ambiguous and bitter-sweet taste left by the laziness of Sundays. As we continued climbing, the impression became more and more pervasive until I stopped at a given moment and looked down towards the end of General Lacy Street where it runs into Ramírez de Prado Street, blocked by the wall of the Railroad Museum that reveals only the undulated roof of its naves and, in the center, the high part of a large factory. It was at that moment that the sensation became more precise and turned into a *vision*: it seemed to me that this was *the end of the city,* that there was nothing further than this except for the suburbs, open areas and the first farming fields that announced the life of the villages and the domain of the woods. As if that wall was *closing* the city, as if it were its natural limit, as if the rest of Arganzuela, Legazpi and further away the M-30 highway and behind the Plaza Elíptica, Usera and the first curves of the highways and their interchanges didn't extend beyond it. Nevertheless, I was aware at that moment that *they did indeed exist,* such that I wasn't hallucinating, but it was as if the sensation of a border that was felt above all else as a *physical* one was imposing itself on the consciousness of the reality of Madrid, determining its own existence and its own *truth.* Of course I was also aware that historically this was actually the limit of the city, but what I was experiencing didn't come from that historic knowledge, but which instead dismissed it as its own possible cause: it wasn't about a historical recollection, rather about an *actualization.* I confided this sensation to my companion who seemed to share it as well. We resumed our walk, and the further upwards we went, the more the perspective became accentuated, and with it the experience of the limit: with the help of the optical illusion I only saw the wall. There wasn't anything behind it; it was the end of the city, and beyond it the beginning of the countryside.

In June of the same year I returned to the Palos de Moguer neighborhood in order to run an errand. Although it was a Saturday morning, its solitary and suggestive atmosphere hadn't changed, and although I didn't reach the wall of the Railroad Museum, I still felt that sentiment, even if attenuated, of reaching the end of the city. On the other hand, the short walk confirmed for me the sensation of being disoriented, of being removed from the points of reference that have

always overwhelmed me when inside the triangle formed by the Paseo de Santa María de la Cabeza, Méndez Álvaro Street and the M-30, a sensation all the more inexplicable when landmarks such as the Atocha railways station or the Paseo de las Delicias with its metaphysical Plaza de Luca de Tena are present. Months later I was talking with my friend Servando Rocha about the psychogeographic interest of this area, and we agreed that it had a special atmosphere that distinguished it from other neighborhoods. As I suggested that this atmosphere could be attributed to the fact that it looks like the end of the city, my friend immediately expressed his agreement, as if that possibility hadn't struck him before, and which only clarified in the best way possible the mystery of the neighborhood. Around the same period of time, I communicated to other friends the sensation of "the end of the city" that I had experienced, which led them to respond by telling me of similar experiences: for Julio Monteverde, the end of the city would be found in the Templo de Debod and for Andrés Devesa in the Parque de la Cornisa, places which could never be the end of *anything*, since streets and buildings are to be found around them as far as the eye can see. It goes without saying that these coincidences filled me with satisfaction for two interconnected reasons: because they seemed to integrate an individual and anecdotal experience into a much wider field, and likewise, importantly, that of collective experience, and also because such a common experience also seems to confirm, on the psychological and sensible levels, serious consideration regarding the death of the city, or at least its nearly fatal crisis, a consideration that *has* to leave the theoretical prison in which it is sometimes confined so as to be utilizable in other ways and with other energies, thus transforming itself into the practical truth of flesh and bone, and therefore as a force of resistance and revolt. And in that sense the mere existence of such a shared sensation would make it possible to animate the hope of this resistance and revolt.

•

If the city – I mean the big city (1) – is dying, it is because it dies of *apparent* success. In reality, the more it imposes its domination, then the more it betrays itself and thwarts its own promises with more force. Thus the bitter victory of the metropolis as both center and sewer of the economy is also a double suicide, a double adulteration that suffocates the very same quality of life in the city, its distinctive features, the qualitatively distinctive experiences that made it possible to assert that the air of the city made us free. Definitely a twice-stabbed heart: on the outer level because the physical expansion of the city (which makes it grow like a cancer through territories more and more extensive and remote from its historic center, putrifying the landscape with the vomited concrete of its commercial centers, highways, rotundas, row-house suburbs, highrises, gas stations and theme parks, apart from being an ecological aberration in and of itself) makes the affective identifications impossible between the man who doesn't know where he lives and the city that has forgotten where it came from and for what it was created. And on the inner level because economic homogenization, with its franchises and commodities, with its renovations and its cultural events, is gradually erasing and denaturing the intimate and characteristic spirit of every neighbourhood and place, turning them into interchangeable aisles of the same supermarket. Therefore the qualitative experience of the city, and we are of course talking in terms of freedom and of poetry, falls into a crisis, which is also the crisis of poetry and the crisis of freedom. Thus, for example, the experience of wandering is being transformed into a search for the gold of time if the city offers from its bosom a sufficient variety of different landscapes, atmospheres, habits, customs and people – a variety that manifests itself from the name of a bar to the objects that the neighbors throw into the street, and which is *evident* as it is only in the city that such simultaneously exquisite and conflicting mixtures can be found that ignite the spark of adventure, of meeting, of desire and of love in the same way that they ignite the fuse of great revolutionary convulsions. But in a city where everything tends to be the same, where the behaviors are stereotyped with the false variety of a commercial catalogue, in an artificial place that doesn't allow itself to be compared with other ways of life, especially with the rural ones, and even less from contact with nature, the ultimate luxury that those lack who think that they have everything, the points of reference and of comparison are thereby lost. And then the experience of the city, poetic or not, remains devoid of meaning, since it isn't a genuine experience in the first place, and then secondly, it cannot be compared (and therefore valued, savored, enjoyed), with other ways of life that are found in a cabin in the woods, at a countryside village or a provincial locality.

In this way the most has defeated the best, in what has generated that *sensation of confinement* (physical, mental, psychological and imaginary) that resides behind the myth of the infinite metropolis without limits, without exits, without alternatives – a quintessentially negative and paralyzing myth, and therefore also revealing of how unrest towards the prevailing civilization makes a place for itself despite everything (2). Enough of this, of course, to suspect that its victory has never been complete, and this text intends to demonstrate that just as other symptoms do more or less – but sufficiently – to break the signals of prohibition that the dominion puts on every corner, in every dream and in every desire (3). That the city retains a part of its vigor and its mystery doesn't negate the fact that the threat of its liquidation into amorphous urbanism and into the biological indifference of the spectacle is still present, each time more subjugating and totalitarian. And we know that it wasn't always like this. Quite the opposite – the city, despite its suburbs that never ceased to form the real and imaginary transition between two worlds (4), had precise limits that distinguished the character of the urban from what extended beyond it: the obscurity of the forest, the insolence of the desert, the solemnity of the mountain, or the enchanting waves of the ocean that invites one on the ultimate voyage. In this way, the limits of the polis were *sacred,* and for that reason it has been said that the walls of the first cities simultaneously had a symbolic function *even before* the rudimentary, military one which always had been attributed to them, marking, in the most physical way, the sacred frontier between the urban community and the rest of the world. But it is not necessary to revisit prehistory, or Greece, or the medieval communes, since much closer to our own historical time period and from those outstanding qualities of the city that interest us, we can find the keys to what we want to say in the symbolist novel, *A Fragment of Life*, by Arthur Machen. Neither is it necessary to insist on how the symbolists are among the first to explore the secret-bearing sphinx of the city, mapping its chameleonic skin that never made it onto the maps of political power and economic law: amorous nostalgia as Hugues Viane's only compass, Strindberg's furious signs, the impossible paths that opened the night to Poictevin the somnambulist… Therefore Machen's little book, published in 1906 and late with respect to symbolism – and precisely because of that delay

– is even more significant as a condensation of that movement and as a bridge towards even more ambitious ones.

Indeed, Edward Darnell, the protagonist of a novel that comes from something deeper and goes much further than literature, discovers that the *real life* (it is Machen who literally uses Rimbaud's magic formula) that abolishes the suffocating mediocrity of an existence of frugality, work, and boredom can emerge from a simple walk through the inconspicuous streets of London, always when it is done with different eyes in order to "feel where nobody had been before." Even better, being lost in the streets of the most civilized city in the world has the unexpected consequence not only of imposing on Darnell the firm belief "that he and all his friends and acquaintances and fellow-workers were interested in matters in which men were never meant to be interested, were pursuing aims which they were never meant to pursue, were, indeed, much like fair stones of an altar serving as a pigsty wall" (no, it doesn't have to do so much with this), but that such a revelation likewise was a preparation to recuperate and *revitalize* the true life of wild nature and to be worthy of it. Thus the walks through a transformed London during a vacation enable Darnell to resuscitate the ancient Celtic myths, the lost relics of the Romans, and the call of the forest, to top it off. What an admirable paradox – when the marvellous found in the industrial city isn't in opposition with the natural, mythical and pre-industrial marvellous, but rather is its *sine qua non* condition so that the latter comes forth from the swollen consciousness of the civilized, an initiatic path that leads from the one to the other because the one is inside the other, because the marvellous is one and indivisible. Therefore the experience of the secret interiority of the city prepares for and corresponds with the experience of exteriority, which for me Machen expresses in the most *marvellous* way in the first – and most intense – of the walks that his improbable hero happily undertakes: when at dawn he leaves his house and "the few known streets" in order to disappear into the ordinary London of common buildings (although now "illuminated by a new light"), until imperceptibly, after walking and walking, following that new light, he reaches the open countryside, the woods and the meadows so that he can stay in a small village on the top of a hill far, *very far from the edge of the city*.

Y entonces, cuando crees que ya no hay camino y te asomas al despiste, una música invisible te atrae hasta la puerta.
¿Dónde están las llaves?

That it was possible to leave London by foot in 1906 to the point of getting lost in the countryside, *and that it is no longer possible today*, is what has been lost, and in this way we have been diminished.

•

Based on these considerations, I decided to see if I could be as worthy of that new light and how far I could get, whether outside of Madrid or at the threshold of its true limit. The following relation is a transcript of the notes taken during the two days that I dedicated myself to such an interior journey (as all true voyages are interior, as everyone knows).

December 2007

I decide to take the subway to the Delicias station, not out of laziness (I live in Lavapiés only two subway stops away), but rather to whimsically get off at that area to explore, thereby searching for (to the extent of what's possible and with such naïve expediency) a certain level of strangeness very convenient for my purposes. After leaving the subway at the Paseo de Las Delicias, I run into the sidewalk opposite the Colegio de Nuestra Señora de las Delicias, made of brick and of a style somewhere between historicist and modern, which looks like a stately mansion or school for the ruling class at the beginning of the 20th century, built on what was once the outskirts of Madrid. Descending through the Paseo de Delicias, I turn left at the first street that I find, Tomás Breton, where there is a cluster of low houses that share the same construction model, i.e. two floors with a higher central body, four windows on the sides and a circular gable with columns, undoubtedly a neighborhood intended for workers of that old manufacturing area and similar to other such neighborhoods that were built in analogous fringes like the Ventas neighborhood. Continuing through Tomás Breton Street, I enter the Alonso Martos alley with more low houses and a yard, which ends with a fenced-in area with a factory wall to the side. The alley is in the process of reconstruction, with restored houses that surely and sadly are destined for *yuppies*, but this fact doesn't prevent the alleyway from appearing as a tiny and wonderful village without the sound of cars but with those of birds instead, and completely deserted. Finally leaving Alonso Martos, I notice that behind # 46 and 42 of Tomás Breton Street, one can contemplate an open field and some factories, or rather, a manufacturing complex from a different era. I continue through Tomás Breton Street until reaching the corner of Turalmina Street and I feel totally perplexed: before my eyes extend large fields with a few housing developments of the latest fashion and living examples of speculation. I leave the desolate field to my left and continue through Tomás Breton Street that turns to the right, descending a steep incline. And so I arrive at #58 where a children's preschool stands decorated with painted phrases on the front: "No adult remembers such a place because memory doesn't exist. Nobody knows how to arrive, but only those who get lost. And then when you think that there still isn't a way and you head towards absentmindedness, an invisible music attracts you towards the door. Where are the keys?" The keys of the city? And I, did I get lost? The wind whips my face as if I were in an open field and indeed, the few buildings and the broad, empty streets do not offer the dubious, artificial protection that makes the city inhabitants believe that nature doesn't exist. Yes, I am lost, and with no sign of the ancient El Águila factory. So I decide to retrace my steps and return to the beginning of Tomás Breton Street, now going down the first street that goes to the right, Batalla de Mar Salado. Thus I meet Watteau Street – narrow, dirty and full of graffiti – more of a venthole or a garage exit than a street, a sordid Cythera to which nobody wants to travel yet is highly suited for being the somber ruin of an industrial sector that *C.S.O. La Traba* doesn't completely succeed in renovating. Finally, Batalla del Mar Salado Street leads me to Plaza Beata Mª Ana de Jesús (*sic*), and this one to Plaza de Legazpi. Both share the same provincial appearance, somewhere between modest and pretentious, between proud and vulnerable, leaning more towards the latter than the former. The appearance of the unavoidable end of the city, reinforced even more in the case of Legazpi by its water-tower, a twin of the one that stands over the place that up until recently had also been a terminal point in Madrid: the Plaza de Castilla. Between the two towers, highly modest and ramshackle masses (but of course much more useful and suggestive than the giants with feet of clay that the economy raises to the greater glory of its obscene pride), the spine of the city stretches: a glowing river of steel, glass and noise.

Well, there is no doubt that I got lost! I take a look at the clock; it is already late and I consider the excursion finished. The end of the city has eluded me, but for the whole time the signs and the smell of its threshold had been all around (5).

January 2008

This time I prefer to make sure of my destination and consult a map, whereupon I take Áncora Street from Paseo de las Delicias, passing some junkyards, formerly an unmistakable symptom of the suburb. At #28, I find a triple archway through which one enters the peculiar and secret Pasaje de Áncora whose false L-shape is completed on its vertical side by a small alley. That side is formed by an old, brick building with a kind of leaning tower in the center, maybe to house a staircase like in the old mansions of Perigueux. Close to the building there is a small garden, and its wall is decorated with scenery reminiscent of the local life of old, proletarian Madrid: low houses, clothes drying on clotheslines, the plaza's fountain. And indeed, the side that forms the alley is closed by a grating that leads to the narrow patio of a whitewashed house. Living more in its own past than the present, a climbing plant ascends the weathered bricks. The last leg of the Pasaje Áncora, which ends at Vara del Rey Street, integrates more suburban, single-floor houses together with "social" buildings from Franco's time and also a few incorporated examples of current, speculative architecture. But apart from the deafening silence that makes it unlikely that this place is situated in the center of Madrid, what fascinates me is the *white light* that has received me and played with me, jumping and following me after I have entered the passage. The light comes from the building with the leaning tower, and I think that it is a mischievous child playing with a mirror, but no, it is only the reflection of a CD that hangs in one of the windows, most likely to scare away the pigeons. Is it from this green ray of light, or this rainbow that the way out of the city or the point where it ends is indicated?(6) I leave the passage and descend through Vara del Rey Street towards the old El Águila factory, once again surprised by the abandoned and naked aspect of the area which is also manifested in something so *abnormal*, just for the mere logic of domination, like the near-total absence of shops except for some bars, bakeries and the

rehearsal studio that my friend Servando's punk rock group frequents: there isn't even a single bank! Finally I reach the old factory and turn through Ramírez de Prado street in order to go up General Lacy Street like in my first visit. I take a look backward and my doubts are fortunately allieviated: even if the sensation isn't as painful, and couldn't be, I again experience that *finis urbis* which is now merged with a certain blend of sanctimoniousness and dead city. Coming to the end of the street I meet up with a big glass building that had caught my attention during the first visit, confirming (without my becoming terribly surprised because indeed in this neighbourhood I'm effectively *lost*), that it was nothing less than the new part of Atocha railways station that serves as a roost for the inauspicious bird, AVE, the high speed train. At the edge of the AVE high speed train terminal, Méndez Álvaro Street goes along in an infinite perspective towards nothing because the end *is not visible*. I finish my walk, directing my gaze one last time at the wall of the Railroad Museum, while thinking of the Wall of the Federados of the Parisian Père-Lachaise cemetery, an association of ideas that I reject immediately as being cliché as well as sinister (weren't people executed there by firing squads during the civil war, or even worse, after it?). I take the way back through Murcia Street, and the first street that crosses it is Rafael de Riego Street (one can see that a late absolutist revenge deprived him of the title of general), that ends also at Ramírez de Prado Street. General Riego perhaps he wasn't *executed by a firing squad* following the Trienio Liberal defeat?

No, I remind myself while writing the present text; Riego wasn't shot, but rather hanged at the Plaza de la Cebada. However, General Lacy *was indeed shot* at Bellver castle in Palma de Mallorca in 1817 after the unsuccessful liberal insurrection that he waged against King Fernando VII (7).

•

When the city seems condemned to vanish into the quicksands of the megapolis, then the ridiculous fires alight and the sound of chains is shaken. Then an invisible figure manifests itself in the sensible like the spirit of the place that shouts the alarm, claiming rights that are ours as well. It is the voice of Madrid's egregore, red and black, that reappears from the ocean of time, avoiding the debris of all the failures so that our ears hear it, so that our voices shout it out. If certain points of Madrid are imbued with the ability to limit, *it is because that limit is necessary*, and it is because the city itself requires a boundary that distinguishes it from the outskirts and which strengthens it in its own essence, preventing its own life from needing assistance, and from devouring all that surrounds it. The cities are doubtlessly growing, and it is absurd to think that what was once near the end would forever remain so: walls are demolished, avenues and boulevards are being built, and then it will be necessary to construct new neighbourhoods for those who come from afar. There is no reason to oppose the *organic growth* that develops according to the natural rhythm of human and urban needs, but not according to the sound of the economy's artificial whistle. Because the economy hates the city just as it hates the world, we have therefore no other remedy than to end it or succumb to it. Therefore the city *needs an end*, some recognizable limits, a carrying-capacity to be determined by nature and the region that surrounds it, so that the autonomy of its inhabitants, the beauty of its streets, the charm of its lost passages and as well as its sanity can again be made possible. It is obvious that the mere idea of *removing* all the fatty tissue that has grown around and from within the city exceeds our abilities, our capacity for action and maybe even that of our imagination. It is of course much easier to consider all the committed evil as irreversible and to be indifferent or fatalistic accomplices, as well. But it is at this point where the experience of the end of the city breaks in with its unreasonable reasons so as to sabotage the common sense of the realism *that conforms*. Those who accept this will have to decide whether they prefer to get lost in it and find their way back to the city that could have been but wasn't, or remain under the order of power until the final implosion.

Post scriptum

Now I realize that I actually have often experienced the end of the city since childhood and maybe from before that. I lived for a long time in Alcalá Street, further down from Plaza de Manuel Becerra, next to the Plaza de Toros, at this strange point of friction between the bourgeois Salamanca neighbourhood and the (then) proletarian or at least artisan Ventas neighbourhood. In Ventas (for a long time the natural limit of the city), my father had always lived, and through him I have known how things were right after the civil war: cow-sheds, workshops, groups of single-storey workers' houses, coquettish small hotels for the lovers of the rich, the house with its beautiful garden of the republican doctor that was requisitioned by the fascist *La Falange*, the Fuente del Berro, the open fields before the fascist expansion of Franco and the mad thirst of the M-30 that swallowed the Abroñigal creek. That atmosphere of the *working-class neighbourhood* could still be appreciated when I was little, as fields and abandoned houses could be found here and there next to Alcalá Street when one entered it from Rufino Blanco; the infamous Women's Prison had already been demolished, and near its enormous lot, an old countryside house with burned walls and a nearly collapsed roof sheltered the strange and dangerous adolescent rituals from which I was excluded and was never able to understand. At the end of the 80's one could still find the relics of the suburb when passing through the alleys that came from Cartagena Street. Thus one morning, under the pretext of conducting an investigation (which I had then dedicated myself to), I entered the large gateway of a neighboring and for the most part nondescript tenement The large courtyard welcomed me by revealing its hidden treasures: cages for chickens, a poultry yard and the workings of a cow barn, miraculously intact, as if sleeping in time, waiting for the new reenchantment that would release them from the malediction of progress, returning them to life. On the other hand, my mother was born during the civil war in the Cuatro Caminos neighborhood, another limit of Madrid, and not only in a geographic or social manner, as it was situated very near the front of the Ciudad Universitaria campus during the fighting. She recalled having visited the trenches after the war – a gloomy frontier or open wound between reality and desire. And further down through Reina Victoria, she said, there were people who still lived in caves. And children were still bathing in the Manzanares. When her only brother died very young, the family took the metro line #2 to Manuel Becerra where they left their grief at the Almuneda cemetery. "The Square of Joy" they called it. The limit between the city of the living and the city of the dead.

1. I am not unaware of the fact that, talking about the metropolis, I am leaving aside the sensible experience of the reality and of the life of the "provincial" cities and of the villages. But I cannot help it as I live in Madrid to begin with and can only talk about my own experience of exteriority, or the lack thereof, which obviously is being determined by this type of city, and secondly, which seems to me much more important, because it is within the big cities (converted into megalopolises or in the process of becoming as such, as is the case with Madrid), that the inhabitants and economic resources of the world become more and more concentrated, with the deplorable consequence that the mentality and the way of life of these enormous urban crowds impose themselves over everything else, deforming the city into its anomalous image. A recent and repugnant advertisement in the subway is the best example of what I mean: a country village in the Third World, in the Phillippines it seems, has decided to build an absurd and ridiculous subway line because one of its inhabitants who has emigrated from Madrid convinced his neighbours that progress, well-being and happiness depend at all costs on being *like the big city.*

2. See in this regard the article by Julio Monteverde, whose origin, like that of this article, was largely inspired by prior discussions which alluded to that sensation of the end of the city.

3. The revitalization of certain neighborhoods through the arrival of immigrants with their own habits and customs which still aren't completely subdued by the ideology of the commodity would be another sure and inspiring example of that continuous reinvention of the city that hasn't yet discovered its last marvels and perhaps never will, to the extent that our thirst for the marvellous is never fully quenched.

4. How well Jacques Prévert, André Thirion and the other surrealists of Château Street knew how to find the non-Parisian's ambiguous magic, the melancholic domain of the vampires of Feuillade, and the sunday *guinguettes*, all within "the lethal boredom of the suburbs."

5. I had in fact been disoriented from the beginning, getting farther and farther away from my goal, which didn't disturb me at all. That I didn't succeed in reaching a place where I had recently been appeared to me as an *umorous* note that moreover strengthened the disorienting character that I ascribe to Arganzuela. After all, perhaps only those who get lost are the ones who arrive?

6. It is only now as I edit the text and sort out the notes that I took during my walks that I realize the analogy that exists between my light and Darnell's new light.

7. I have preferred to limit to an essential minimum the historical inquiry regarding the places that I visited. Such an investigation would undoubtedly bring forth new facts and surprises, and maybe this would be necessary if we were to speak about establishing affective and visionary connections through time within a specific space, but I prefer to leave it for the moment so as not to alter the strictly spontaneous character of the experience.

Eyes of Water

Silvia Guiard

This piece features two approaches to a vision of a particular place. The first, called "The Blue Cape," is a sort of interior exploration that occurred spontaneously in me in 1986. If I include it here, despite its marked introspective tone (which might sound strange in a project devoted to exteriority) it was inspired by the following fragments from a text by Eugenio Castro, *Surrealism and Exteriority*: "What landscape or landscapes, besides those elements already mentioned, and which display such a tangible aspect, would embody this absolute presence and could indicate – each one according to its *fall* into them – their mouth of shadow," Eugenio writes, adding that, entering through them into nature, "we can begin to unravel part of our own mystery, in the very fabric of correspondences," by means of "a gaze that expands the coordinates of the relationship between external and internal life, taking its dialogue as far as possible." It's here that "The Blue Cape" can be situated: it concerns precisely an exploration of the correspondences within a series of internal experiences that led me to discover the magical character that a place in the Andes I visited in my childhood had for me. That I visited? Or should I say it was the place that visited me and continues to visit me? Who looks at whom when we lean over the water?

"The Blue Cape"—which I transcribe here unchanged save for the addition of a couple of notes—proclaims its orientation toward an exploration of time, and is effectively a kind of descent into the concentric circles of dream and memory. But at its center is this particular place, which is double, and an element: water.

1

THE BLUE CAPE

It all began the 25th of May of '86 when I wrote a poem, immedi-

-ately called THE ENCHANTED CHILD.

There are passageways, there always have been,
Where those strange gestures, the fragments of gestures
Which form us, are repeated.
The deep labyrinths of memory:
Do I always return to another place? Which one?
Why did I dream about the malones? (1)
Why did that gallop, wild and spectral, traverse my childhood?

The house that burns down at midnight: everything trembles
There's a black hallway that's crossed at a gallop, with eyes closed
And the eye of fascination: an eye of water
quiescent, green, mysterious, transparent,
an eye in the palm of my hand
a mouth of shadow
among the stones

– You arrive there among dreams:
it's a high and solitary place
a small cave, damp and dark
and the face of a virgin trembles among candles
everything trembles
and the eye of the Secret
blinks
It's the Enchanted Child
the girl with green, transparent eyes
with her mute mouth open
forever in the palm of my hand –

It's fascination
which is blinking

I see myself walk away over the sand
among the eddies of memory
hunter of tentative eyelids

gnawing my life
amid the catapult of dead
And maintaining thus my own blood
against wind and tides
in the desert!

I'm tied by my hair
to the thread of my voice

Return to what place? And from where?
At night
I put on the eyes of the dead
and with my black body
I dance in the half-light
with the Giants
The cones of shadow know me
the sleepy cusps of the moon
the white rattles
the chimes mad with laughter:
because I, I'm alive,
and amidst the dead!

The jagged blue of my dress
scatters like mist over the earth
Would the Woman, darkened by her shadow,
who called My Name, have lived, then, someday?

What is, I wonder, the Time of Life?

Poetry
is born near silence
like sleep

It turns in spiral
around a secret place
a sacred spot
like in dreams

Around the eye of water
Of Mystery

The Child's body?
My own body?
Am I the actual victim plunged
within the profound waters of enchantment
and is it with my own body
that I weave between my lips
the Legend?

Around a small black chest
Sealed and gleaming
-a little coffin-
life is born

I saw the stone fall
into the still iris of the waters
and swimming
I speak
in concentric circles

ECHOES OF THE ENCHANTED CHILD

Once again, through "the deep labyrinths of memory" I stand before the Lagoon of the Enchanted Child. Veritable *eye of water* lost among the mists of time and dreaming, in its shell of silence this place holds one of my oldest experiences of the Marvelous. I went there when I was very young. It's in Mendoza, where my parents are from, and where we went every summer and to which I felt passionately attracted. It's a deep, natural well opened in the mountain, almost perfectly round. And there She lies at the bottom, several meters below: Water.

A transparent, motionless water: sleeping. Her image and the legend evoked by her name have fascinated me ever since.

Beside the lagoon there's a small grotto converted into a sanctuary:

the figure of a virgin, flowers, candles, the penumbra charged with the beating of wings and my own experience of the Secret, the Sacred.

The lagoon opens before me the revelation of a prodigious profundity unlike few others: the concentric circles around a sinking stone. And here as well, or in some other place close by in space, in time or in memory: the magnetism of echoes.

From echo to echo, much later my fascination would reach the edge of Mexico's sinkholes. Here as well, beside the offerings of ritual gold, maidens open eyes anaesthetized by time and surrender themselves to the water…

The water, death, rites, sacrifice: everything is there, spinning around, and implicates me. But what ritual? Who knows? I know that I had the impression, when writing the poem, that this was just the beginning of a long process referring to—revolving around—the Time of Life, which would "knot" a new cycle, just like the ancient Mexicans knotted each cycle/century that just ended.

DREAM ON THE NIGHT OF 26/05/86

We're in the water: muddy, murky, limitless. The shores are invisible. The water reaches up to my chest. I'm there, behind me Sony (2), and further back a third person unidentified during the entire dream. We're beneath the pylons of a pier: thick wooden posts, dark, covered with algae. I'm carrying a baby in my arms. Apparently it's Sony's son; in any case it's a boy. I'm extremely worried about the possibility that the baby could drown (I know that the depth increases just a few steps further out), and I have no desire to have this responsibility in my arms. Meanwhile I'm thinking: "I always wanted to know how it felt to give birth, but now it's all happened so fast that I don't remember a thing." I remain anxious, and I'm trying to convince someone else to take the baby, but Sony doesn't seem to understand my apprehension. Suddenly, something happens, it's like a gust of wind: the baby falls into the water. As the water is murky, I think I have to pull him out blind, with my hand, by his hair. I plunge my hand into the water, but I can't find him. I submerge myself, but I don't dare open my eyes. I open them for an instant: it's all muddy. The baby doesn't appear. Sony is quite calm. All of a sudden we see the baby in the sky. That's when I realize that we will no longer find him in the water, that he's died. This is what we see: the sky is very blue; the moon is invisible, but not its light; it's as though the moon were a projector placed behind the sky that permitted us to see the baby against the light; or more precisely, four white figures in the form of ovoids. They could be illustrations showing the development of the fetus or the phases of the moon. Only the third one is sharp: the fetus, wrapped in its transparent sack, floats placidly. It's a very beautiful image. We continue to look at the sky. The image changes: now there's a wooden table (to the left) and beside it two elderly men who look like monks or (jovial) alchemists and an adolescent, nearly pubescent (it's the baby, now grown) who looks like a medieval apprentice, dressed in a light blue cape and with his hair down to his shoulders. The old men give him instructions and hand him a map and a watch (a map of the city of Buenos Aires and a cheap quartz watch). We realize that this means he will be coming down to Earth, to be with us. The watch is set to a special hour, that has something to do with the child (a little past noon, apparently two in the afternoon). Sony says, "He's perfect." I insist, "But can't you see that he's dead?" I don't think he understands what's going on. I submerge myself once again. Despite the murky water, I see a kind of large, transparent glass bubble, resting on the river bottom which is sandy and soft here. It's all incredibly beautiful: the inside of the bubble is decorated with corals and starfish. Everything is clear and beautiful. The baby should be there, but he isn't. When I come to the surface I think, "Despite everything, we can be proud to have such a pretty place for our babies."

AFTER THE DREAM (26-27 of 05/86)

As soon as I wake up in the morning I enter into a state in which sleep and wakefulness seem to fuse: I have access to memories from conscious life, but I can think with the immediacy, simultaneity and speed typical of dreams. The images that appear have the force of evidence and are accompanied by an extraordinary feeling of lucidity.

So I automatically call the dream "*Immersion before birth. The death which is not death.*" And I know that behind it there's a concrete

experience from my childhood: having fallen when I was two or three into a swimming pool which was being drained and which contained very dirty water, from which my father immediately rescued me. Before he pulled me out of the water, however, I opened my eyes and instinctively began swimming underwater. I retained a visual memory of it for many years: my arms extended before me, the murky water, frogs.

The images that appear in the sky refer perhaps to fantasies or images experienced in the water. I recall, in fact, that I told my mother that I had dreamed "that I reached the sky and that the door was opened for me."

I remember then the poem of the Enchanted Child, and I realize that this dream seems to respond to its questions: I know the place I'm returning to and I know that it's actually my own body that lies "enchanted" in the waters of the lagoon. In fact, I was there not long after my fall and I realize that the indelible impression that the place made on me could be related to the distress which I must have felt in the water, distress which my identification with the enchanted child—not dead but transformed in this extremely beautiful water—changed into a sensation as pleasurable as it was profound: the Marvelous.

Says Pichon-Rivière "...the marvelous is the antithesis [of the sinister]. They are two feelings linked in a profoundly dynamic way. And one is the overcoming of the other. That is, when one is dominated by the sinister and manages to overcome this distressing painful state, the marvelous emerges as an expression of tranquility" (3).

Thus, the dream came to reveal the key to one of my first poetic impressions and, perhaps, that "mouth of silence open / forever in the palm of my hand": Poetry. It came to reveal which secret ritual—the ritual of *transfiguration*—was celebrated for me "around mystery's eye of water" where, the poem states, poetry is born, like a dream.

But apart from that, what was the dream about? It seems to take up once again the poem's query: what is the Time of Life? The baby is and is not me, it is and is not my son, he died, but has yet to be born. The water and the sky represent his death, and at the same time the uterus, the place previous to birth... While I'm turning all this over in my mind, I suddenly recall another recent dream and look for my record of it. When I reread it, I'm utterly surprised by the close connection with the poem of the 25th and the dream of the 26th, both by the elements that appear and by my transcription of it.

Here it is: "I'm at the edge of the cliff and I'm thinking about the crime. How easy it is to kill, I say to myself, and hide the evidence. It's a narrow path with rickety handrails at the edge of a 200-meter chasm. The sea is pounding furiously below and the spray off its waves reaches me, filling everything with a gray mist. Am I about to fall? Is it my body that's to be offered to death with no proof whatsoever? These deep, purple jaws before me… Who could judge me? Then something occurs in the air, to my left, like a fluttering announcing the presence of something. I turn around: immense, wrapped in a blue cape, standing on the stony hillside, is my dead father (who I know is dead). At first I'm afraid, but this feeling changes rapidly. Papa opens an immense black umbrella and starts spinning it in front of him: it's a gesture with a meaning, directed at me."

It's apparent that both dreams recount the same story from opposite perspectives. Here, the enormous presence of my father puts me in the place of a child: it's me who is going to fall. (…) And the enigmatic link with this mysterious blue cape that, from one dream to another, transforms the dead father into a child about to be born, not to mention the poem where "the jagged blue of my dress / scatters like mist over the earth…"!

But there's much more here: because in this *transmutation* of the father into the child, of death into birth, from murkiness to clarity, of the sinister into the marvelous, in this effort of transmutation of the Time of Life, silence has been transmuted into words and has been revealed as poetry.

A magical event, a ritual of transfiguration undoubtedly presided over by the Moon, the old Our Lady of the Dead, but also of fertility, who governs the rhythms of life an its eternal regeneration.

"At night
I put on the eyes of the dead
and with my black body
I dance in the half-light
with the Giants
The cones of shadow know me

the sleepy cusps of the moon
the white rattles
the chimes mad with laughter:
because I, I'm alive,
and amidst the dead!"

Something in my ears tends to transport the "white rattles" upwards, to replace the "sleepy cusps" and produce "white rattles of the moon." And that is where I feel the most vivid intensity or poetic condensation: in this image anticipating the fusion that would occur in the dream between the four phases of the moon and the development of the fetus. Its precisely at this moment, which is also the dream's most beautiful part, when anguish turns to pleasure (the contemplation of a marvelous image) and then, after the magical intervention of the ancients-alchemists-ancestors-deceased(?), the lost baby is transformed into the child about to be born, the dream now divided into two parts: that of the first immersion in the turbid, distressing, disgusting water, and the second immersion, with the apparition of the transparent, beautiful, bright bubble. It's the same transformation produced in that fragment of the poem, where the identification of the moon with the white rattles permits the passage from darkness (night-the dead-black-shadows) to the clarity of the "chimes of laughter" to conclude in the victorious affirmation: *"because I, I'm alive, and amidst the dead!"*

So that's the experience of '86 (4). Now I'd like to return to the places evoked, in order to question them. There are two. I confirmed much later that in '86, my memory combined two places located in the same valley, near to each other and always visited together: the Lagoon of the Enchanted Child, with its emerald green water and small grotto, and the Well of Spirits. In this well, similar to Mexico's sinkholes, where the surface of the water—no less green and transparent—is "various meters below."

But what exactly are these places in themselves? What did my infantile vision capture there that could produce such fascination?

2

These places, geology tells me in the first place, are *dolinas*, karstic formations consisting of soft terrain (in this case gypsum, in others limestone), in which both subterranean waterways and surface currents that filter downward, dissolve the rocks, opening enormous underground caverns. The surface terrain finally gives way, forming sinkholes in the form of cones. If vegetation secures the well walls, the process stops; if not, it remains active and the cones continue to grow (5).

It's the water that creates. The water above and the water below work together to form these places.

Standing at the surface, embracing with a single glance the whole of the sky and the surrounding hillsides, and simultaneously all the depths there below, there inside—and it's *80 meters* down: the vertigo of the depths of the earth. That's the experience of being at the edge of the Well of Spirits. (Visitors toss stones from the top to see how long they take to fall. "You look from outside," writes Eugenio Castro (6). Maybe so, but falling toward the inside, as the stone falls.)

A motionless place, but still vertiginous towards the depths and towards the heights; how could the vertical of time not unfold within it, traversing it?

A motionless place? Still waters, yes, but sleeping in a well that grows at every instant, in a terrain that gives way day by day. Aren't these cones, with their walls collapsing downward, like giant sand clocks?

It's water and time that together realize this labor of erosion.

But time itself, whether running or at rest, what is it but water? "Because we're in the water, in the misty water of dreams, in the water of time," I wrote elsewhere about "The Blue Cape."

"The past of our souls," Gastón Bachelard says, "is deep water"(7). And here, in these places, what pasts, what dreams, what souls are reflected? It's enough to pronounce their names in order to know that they are places that *dream*. The notion of legends is so consubstantial with them that you could say they were "event-places." They imply stories. Hence, the place whose name and individual presence I had forgotten in '86, the Well of Spirits—which owes its name to the peculiar way the wind has of howling around it—was, however, subterraneously present in the content of the dream and my subsequent reflections, impregnating

them with its meaning. The "spirits" which the popular imagination hears moaning in this well, are they dead? Or just waiting to be reborn?

I visited it again in January of 2000, 26 years after last setting foot in Mendoza. Alone and on foot, I had no other way to reach the valley from the closest city than to rent a car with a guide exclusively for me. A 19-year-old local, a man-boy who took me where I had never been before: descending along a zigzagging trail to the bottom of the well, right at the water's edge. My guide introduced himself by his nickname: Cali. Of course, "Kali;" who else could have accompanied me in this way on my descent to the depths of the earth. But there was nothing terrible about his aspect or in the adventure of our descent. We remained down there a long time, in a free exercise of childhood: tossing stones into the water or watching tiny boats made from twigs as they floated away. Or waiting to spot the ripples which suddenly spread across the water, like the tremors that flutter across the back of a sleeping animal when he dreams. No, seen up close the water is not completely motionless. If it sleeps, then it dreams. There are imperceptible gusts that abruptly form a current of small waves: they move swiftly toward one side and dissolve. After a while, unpredictably, ripples scurry in another direction and become still once again. It's as though a cluster of tiny hands were pushing the water here and there from below in some random game. Or as if invisible creatures were flying above the water, brushing it with the tips of their feet and leaving a wake. The spirits must be, like we ourselves, simply children playing.

The local legend, however, speaks of warriors. Of a group of natives who, while pursuing their enemy through the night, became trapped in the well when the earth collapsed beneath their feet. The natives called the place *Trolope-co*, "water of the shrieking dead." Now the locals claim that all the souls wandering the mountains in pain come here to weep. And what souls would these be?

Trolope-co is a Mapuche word. Why was I so surprised in 2000 when I discovered that all the local place names were in this language? Why, when I knew that this region, Malargüe (*or Malal-hue*) to the south of Mendoza, had formed part of the fierce indigenous resistance? Nonetheless, I hadn't even considered that this valley, these "eyes of water" that had looked at me so deeply in my childhood, had been, precisely, inland (8).

Here I am then, falling once again. I began by evoking something as familiar as my childhood vacations and here I am falling once again into this otherness that makes me shudder, inland, in time, falling. And the entire valley trembles in my memory when I pronounce the word "warriors."

Who were they? Pehuenches (9).

The Spanish crown never conquered these lands.

As early as the 16th century the first *conquistador* to pass through Malargüe discovered a fearsome people, ready to join the resistance of their brothers on the other side of the mountains. Were they Pehuenches? Those who inhabited the area in the 18th century were. They were proud and independent, but with the thorn of the occident already stuck in the center of their *piuke*, or heart: war (10). They fought, but not only with the Spanish authorities (who ended up recognizing their sovereignty in the Parliament of Lonquilmo), but also with their rivals, the Huilliches. They defended a territorial strategy that, by dominating the mountain passes, extended to the east as far as the *pampas* and from which they forged links, both diplomatic and commercial, with the colonial government in Mendoza as well as with the Chillán, in Chile, and other branches of the Mapuche in Patagonia and the Pampa. Powerful warriors, agile horsemen and magnificent weavers, they exported their *ponchos* to Santiago, Mendoza, Córdoba, Buenos Aires and Asunción… Here is where they lived.

And this valley, "my valley," carved by the Chadileufú or Río Salado, whose mouth, further downriver, was settled by various native villages; this valley, frozen in winter but which in times of abundant pastures attracted groups from both sides of the mountains who passed the summer here; this luminous and transparent valley where life came and went, busy with encounters and reunions, was also at one time the site of battles, a region of "cries and commotion"(11), raids and attacks, resistance, cavalry charges, alliances, parliaments, treachery, ambushes and death.

Who are the souls that come, then, to cry at the well, if not those of the *loncos* or Pehuenche chiefs? Their shades must be crying hereabouts and now I'd like to speak their names: Peignapil, Ancaluan, Gaiquillan, Guanchupan, Nobuluení, Buenomillia, Umiganqui, Antemanqui, Millamain, Llanquel, Ancan Amun, Pinchitur, Currilipi …

Will the cone of the *dolina* turn upside down one day, like a water clock, so that time will run again for them, *backwards...*?

Why not? They know well that the *wallmapu chuwüzküley*, "the universe turns eternally," they know that the road of life upon the *wallontu mapu,* the Earth, is circular.

A circle alive with energies, forces or *newen*, is the universe for the Mapuches. And what *newen* there are here: both deep below and above. It's easy to imagine how it would be special for them, a sacred place. Because the three principle levels of the world converge here: *Minche mapu* or "the earth beneath," *Naq mapu*, the ground we tread, and *Wenu mapu*, or "the earth above..." Here the *kultrunes* would have sounded, here they would have held ceremonies, solemn prayers, *ngillipunes...* They would still be wandering here, holding ceremonies in the night or letting loose their war cries in the wind, their *afafan*. Yes, it must be them shouting, plunged into the unconscious of a country which has done nothing but deny them (12).

From *Trolope-co*, then, I arrive at the Lagoon of the Enchanted Child and I decide to ask him in his own language: "Chem...?" Who? Who is it that lies here?

It's *Ülcha* (or *Elcha*). So it's not a little girl, since *Ülcha* means: maiden, young girl, virgin. And it's not the same virgin whose effigy one sees today near the water: it's not one of those who says, "I'm the master's slave." To the contrary, her mark is also that of rebellion, resistance. Hers is another kind of war: the kind fought in the name of love, in zealous defense of desire, and against a paternal prohibition that has, moreover, the force of "law."

The story has many variations, but with a single meaning: *Ülcha*, daughter of a *lonco*, refuses to accept the marriage that for diplomatic reasons has been arranged for her with the *lonco* of a rival clan. Her heart has already chosen another, a young man from her village, and she convinces him to elope. They flee. They're pursued, and just when they reach the highest part of the lagoon, they realize they've been overtaken. Before they can be caught, they throw themselves with a single leap from the rim of rock into the frigid water.

It's moving to think how many native legends contain the seeds of a similar tale of love. Sometimes the obstacle is death, or in others, like here, a conflict with social or political conventions. It's as though love, in its struggle to express itself, created forms and places. In nearly all these stories the final supernatural intervention favors the lovers. In this case, against their pursuers. It was the *machi* —female shamans— who advised the marriage and who led the pursuit. But just as the lagoon appears before her eyes, a bolt of lightening falls from the sky, transforming her into stone. And she can still be seen there, in the form of a huge black rock that juts out, threateningly, from the top of the knoll, over the water where *Ülcha* sleeps.

She is also known as *Ülcha of the green tunic*. Green or blue, depending on how the sun hits it, the cloak covering her is adorned with yellow flowers and allows us to see her profound heart. To see her is to drink: water of dreams, transparent liquor.

On moonlit nights things happen: some say that the face of *Ülcha* appears on the water's surface; others say that she awakens and walks on the water to meet her lover, or that you can hear the two of them moaning, pleading for someone to return them to life.

The water produces dreams, images, tales. And according to another legend, mermaids come to sit on the rocks and comb their golden hair when no one is looking (13).

Dreaming here is slow, not dizzying. Deep, yes, but calm, intimate, enveloping. The trembling of stars at night.

The solitary Indian who passed by here would have sat down to think, sing, contemplate. To love.

In this lagoon and in the story of *Ülcha*, the Pehuenche heart, dense with battles, would have had its counterpart in transparency: here masculine power would have reached its internal limit, not in fragility, but in delicacy; here blood would have found its opposite in pure water, turbulence its repose, fierceness its sensitivity.

This is not just an image game. *Ülcha* is not just the name of a character in a legend. It's also a sacred spiritual principle. Its one of the four principles that order the Mapuche universe, one of the four aspects that all *newen* implicates and which are, in this order: *Kuse* (The Old Woman), *Vuta Chao* (The Great father or Old Man), *Ülcha* (The Young Woman), *Weche* (The Young Man). The harmony of the world depended on the equilibrium among this tetrad.

The imbalance that, even before its ultimate victory, the West inflicted on a universe thus conceived, unleashed a state of permanent war that during 350 years gave primacy to the warrior values of the *Weche* and the authority of *Vuta Chao*; this imbalance is the same one that the patriarchal Occident bore and continues to bear in its interior.

The lagoon used to be known as *Alwe pichi trenguen lauquen*; something like "small lake of the spirit which freezes." How could *Ülcha* not become frozen, how could she not cry until she turned to stone (as one version of the legend has it) seeing the profound disorder which the war provoked among her people, and, after the final victory, in the world that they had lived in? The same disorder that the West suffers and scattered in all directions.

I inevitably imagine, then, that it was something of the voice of *Ülcha* which André Breton captured when, on the shores of another lake, evoking another siren, another war—and even another child drowned in frigid waters—asked: "Who will return the sensitive scepter to the woman-girl?... I think it's within her, and only within her that that other prism of vision resides in a state of absolute transparency but which is stubbornly excluded from consideration, since it obeys very different laws, and whose diffusion masculine despotism must prevent at all costs"(14).

But here in the lagoon, still, all the transparency, all the sacred mystery that *Ülcha* implies is offered, by itself, naturally, with full hands.

And offerings are made. It's true, that "grotto" whose memory moved me in my childhood is there, but it's nothing but a crude artificial structure—although protected by a natural cavity—and in which another virgin seems to receive prayers. But she is as much an intruder here as the construction that shelters her.

Neither the Mapuches nor any of the other native groups that settled the vast territory which is now Argentina, ever erected any kind of temple. Their ceremonies unfolded in the open. Sacredness emanated by itself from nature. A stone, a stream, a mountain, a tree: all embodied a *pillan*, a spirit, a sacred force. That's why it wasn't just minds the Church attempted to vanquish, but the whole territory: everything must, in unison, recite the Lord's Prayer (15). There was no place that didn't require an exorcism against the preexisting "demons;" no mountaintop is today without its cross; no lagoon or grotto without its virgin, as if to cover and silence by insistence the spirits, the presences, the forces that emanate from another time. From another world.

Which is, in reality, the same world. This world in itself.

Still today, in the province of Mendoza but also further north, I've noticed with emotion that any small opening in the cliff walls, any cleft or cavity, is enough for someone to leave candles or flowers there. To whom are they directed? Who do they want to talk to? What hunger do they express? It's as though every crack or hollow in the rock were an object of love, as if every fissure opening toward the other side, unfathomable, toward the interior, were a channel of communication or a path toward Another Place which we still intuit, long for, desire.

Who cares if sometimes there's an image there. It's not that that is observed, but "something else" beyond it. What?

I've never asked anyone anything about it, I've only seen what's there: the flowers of love offered to the Great Cleft in the earth, vulva-eye-mouth of silence, the original Great Cleft.

●

From what depths does the word come? The one that appears in the poem, in the verse that I highlighted among all the others: In Argentina *sonajeros* (rattle) normally designates a sonorous baby's toy, and that's how I thought of it when associating it with the images in my dream. But *sonajeros*, I see now, are also the gourds that the *machi* use, along with the strokes of the *kultrun*, to induce a shamanistic ecstasy and journey, with eyes covered, to the spirit world. Who but *Ülcha*, become *machi*, become *Kuse*, could say, then, these strange words: "At night / I put on the eyes of the dead / and with my black body / I dance in the half-light / with the Giants"? Couldn't the following phrase be put before this strophe (and before the previous and subsequent ones): "*Ülcha* speaks:…"?

How, then? What is this otherness (this other-era) in my throat? Maybe every word is in itself a mouth of shadow, deep towards the depths and towards the heights. That poetic speech, full of eyes, is of water. And in the water I am myself and the other at the same time because whoever looks at the water, says Jung, no doubt sees their own image, but beneath it other living beings soon emerge: fish, but also water nymphs, "an even more instinctive level of a female being which we call animus"(16).

And because water "*crosses* images," says Bachelard (17). And in the "misty waters of dreams," all times merge.

Buenos Aires,December, 2007

---

1. The native word "malón" designates the indigenous attacks on white settlements, but actually, the Indians used first used it to refer to white incursions into their territory.
2. Nickname for a friend whose recently born baby girl I had met a few days before the dream.
3. This citation, taken from Vicente Zito Lema's book *Conversations with Enrique Pichon-Rivière*, is in fact part of the material that contributed to the contents of the dream. I was reading this book in the days previous and in the poem it's already indirectly present. Pichon-Rivière emigrated from France with his family while still a child and he lived first in Chaco. At the time, according to his account in the book, *malones* were still common *and he frequently dreamed about them*. It's as though when writing the poem I had been thinking: "Pichon-Rivière had his reasons, but why did *I* dream of the malones?" Furthermore, in his stories about his childhood there is a very strong presence, almost oneiric, of water, since he describes the massive flooding of the Chaco plains, as well as a childhood excursion to the Iberá Lagoon, and the mysterious *legends* centering on it.
4. Actually, it was just the beginning. The blue cape once again came to affect me (and in what a way) when three years later certain events in "real life" coincided with its images, reinvesting them with meaning. But this is not the moment to speak about it.
5. I said that I had merged two places into one. But the Well of Spirits is in itself double: two depressions separated by a fragile wall (whose disappearance is inevitable). The erosion of one of the sinkholes has stopped, with the walls covered in vegetation. The other, the most impressive due to its size and its sheer walls, measures approximately 200 meters in diameter, drops 80 meters to the surface of the water and 21 more from the surface to the bottom.
So there weren't two but three water mirrors that my memory merged into one.
As for the Enchanted Child, some attribute a volcanic origin and other describe it as a *dolina*. It's surrounded by rocks from a nearby volcano.
6. Eugenio Castro, "Surrealism…" Having cited Eugenio on this point, it's necessary to mention the "concerting" (as opposed to disconcerting) effect of learning that one of the principle karstic formations of limestone on the Iberian Peninsula is… "his" Torcal de Antequera.
7. Gaston Bachelard, *Water and Dreams*, Mexico, FCE, 1978.
8. This is what the Europeans called the territory remaining under Indian control until the end of the 19th century, and is also the title of a piece I wrote on the subject, also in 1986 (see *Tierra Adentro, Salamandra* #15/16, 2005-06, p. 104).
9. A group of the Mapuche nation (or Araucana, as the Spanish conquistadors called them).
10. The equilibrium of Mapuche society, which had no central authority, was based on the coexistence of mutually independent communities. The arrival of the conquistadors broke this balance. On the one hand, by pushing them south in Chile, it generated competition for territory. On the other, it introduced possibilities for the accumulation of power and wealth, be it through war or through alliances with colonial powers. This, combined with the emulation of western individualism, produced a desire in some *loncos* (chiefs) for their own political or military careers, that other *loncos* saw as endangering the traditional ways of

life, and so forming alliances to combat them. Hence, there arose struggles among different groups on the Chilean side, and the victors crossed the frontier in search of new lands to settle to the east of the Andes, uniting familial or friendly groups already living here, or sometimes, fighting with preexisting groups.

11. A phrase taken from a contemporary letter (end of the 18th century).

12. And in my dream, was my father also a suffering soul wandering among the mountains? Perhaps: he had always wished to return to the land that he left in his youth, but died having never made it.

13. There is still another, more recent story about a cunning Chilean who made seven bets with the devil in this place, and beat him.

14. André Breton, *Arcane 17,* New York, Brentano's, 1945.

15. Thus did missionaries, then historians, obstinately try to make *Vuta Chao* synonymous with God, distorting the original fourfold cosmology.

16. C.G. Jung, *The Archetypes and the Collective Unconscious*. The emphasis is his.

17. Op cit: p. 86. The emphasis is his.

Surreality and Exteriority

Eugenio Castro

Aperture. The Delirium of Absolute Presence.

During a trip to Tenerife, in the course of his climb to the 'summit of Teide,' which crowns the Valley of Orotava, André Breton exclaimed: "I regret having discovered these ultra-sensitive regions of the earth so late in life." We shouldn't overlook the motives behind his statement, a series of discoveries provided by certain specific aspects of nature, which he describes in a text whose lyricism, although belatedly indebted to a certain exaltation of the absolute sublime typical of revolutionary romanticism, presages a relationship with exteriority, at least in its latent state. That at least is the idea put forth in this document.

Let's recall beforehand some of those admirable discoveries that led him to express himself in these terms: "Between the martyred blooms of the cacti...here a hundred-branch chandelier of a spurge with a stem as thick as your arm but three times longer, which, hit by a stone, bleeds abundantly white and stains...Little children take delighted aim at this plant from far off, and it must be admitted that the secretion exposed in this way is the most disturbing thing imaginable" (André Breton, El amor loco, p. 71, Joaquín Mortiz, México, 1978). Referring in the same text to "the garden of four seasons of the Orotava," and after expressing wonder at the Dracaena, "this princess lavish with palms," he writes: "Scarcely have we entered then all the little geniuses of childhood throw themselves around our necks. From a little transforming flower, our very learned guide Mr. Bolinaga, presiding over the development of all this display, did not, in fact, disdain to have the rabbit from *Alice in Wonderland* leap forth under our eyes, and it is Alice's dinner table unrolling as far as the eye can reach before us when we had raised to our mouth the Lilliputian tomato of *pitanga*, with the exquisite taste of poison." And referring to its "leaf darted with silk," he declares: "think of what an exorbitant present that would be: bursting forth from a rather small earth pot, a love letter written in this way..." Following this, he can't resist being amazed at another "autochthonous species, I think, of *sempervivum* which enjoys the frightening property of continuing to develop under any conditions...: crumpled, pierced, torn, burned... this glaucous scale, about which you cannot decide if it would be better finally to press it against your heart or to insult it... It tries, at the price of whatever revolting efforts, to reconstruct itself according to the destroyed probabilities that it has. It is lovely and confusing like human subjectivity.... It is no less lovely, no less ineradicable than today's currently desperate will that can be termed *surrealist* just as well in the domain of particular sciences as in the domain of poetry and arts, operating at each moment the synthesis of the rational and the real, without fearing to place in the word "real" everything irrational it can contain *until further notice*." Neither can I avoid mentioning the impression that the light of the *datura* had on him: "All that remains of the light seems produced by the far-off lamps, too white in color, of the *datura*... The quality of this light makes it less bearable than would be its absence in such a place. You think you see evening dresses hanging in the air, dazzling in their pallor. In the depths of the day or the night, no matter which, it's something like the immense vestibule of physical love as one would wish to make it without interruption." Breton finishes with an expression that defines both his mood and his discovery: "The delirium of absolute presence."

Everything in this account indicates (and without touching on the fact that everything consubstantial to it evokes expressions of *amour fou*) that we find ourselves first and foremost before a confirmation of the idea of surreality that the author himself defined in *Surrealism and Painting*: "All that I love, all that I think and feel inclines me towards a particular philosophy of immanence according to which surreality will reside in reality itself and will be neither superior nor exterior to it. And conversely, because the container shall be also the contained. One might almost say that it will be a communicating vessel placed between the container and the contained..."

Nonetheless, it's quite right to agree that this notion (surreality), in this case, has abandoned the city (and urban life), which would seem to be its 'natural' domain, cognizant that it was above all 'cultural.' In fact, it would be correct to acknowledge that *the potential for surreality* has made itself felt in the open here, with unusual and novel energy. Even though there exists, in our opinion, a substantial difference in this experience of surreality, consisting of the fact that it was already out there, and of which we had no previous knowledge through the process of language, so what rises to the surface to crystallize via experimentation with the word is not a "profound emanation," wherein images of *below* acquire physicality. What becomes relevant with respect to the experience of surreality in the open, resides in the fact that access to the unconscious is produced at the surface, by means of a gaze that has captured the *mouth of shadow* of its objects and elements in their absolute presence. (One observation: nothing indicates in what I vindicate that one may at all want to establish any dichotomy.)

This aspect is what determines the new relationship to be established with the notion of surreality, since it induces a movement away from what is known and accepted within the framework of surrealism, a movement that doesn't deny the former, but which does demand its independence, in a reciprocal liberating movement. In this sense, it's easy to understand that, at a time when human spirit (both individual and collective), is undergoing tremendous trauma and evident exhaustion, the force with which exteriority penetrates it might end up exercising an unexpected renewal of that same spirit.

Breton's experience of Teide is, in my opinion, characteristic of one of these moments. The same thing crystallizes in another passage of the text we're examining, where the author refers to his discovery of the black sand beaches and the wonder they produce in him. He declares: "All the shadow cast over the sea is made of the great stretches of even blacker sand which make up so many beaches…" This marvelous state is displayed here in one of his most moving phrases: "Just the reverse of what was for me at fifteen the limit of what I could hope for, to set out for the unknown with a woman at dusk on a white road, I sense today all the emotion of the physical goal attained by treading the unknown with the one I love, the magnificent flowerbed the color of the time when I used to imagine that the tuberose was black."

In a state of falling in love, the poet has relinquished himself, has been exorcised, has gone so far outside himself that the encounter with what exists outside him has revealed itself with all the hope of childhood intact, when life still unfolds for one marvelously lost, and presents itself, in places like La Orotava or Teide, in those years, to the man-boy, in his "delirium of absolute presence," when in this kind of place "the great moral and other contructions of adults, founded as they are on the glorification of effort, of heavy labor, are endangered. Livelihood we call "earned" returns to the aspect it had for us in childhood: it takes on once more the character of a life wasted." (A. Breton, op. cit.). The breakdown of thought must be *powerful*, pointing it toward rugged climes, not toward shady paths. Shouldn't we interpret such an expression as a need to learn the terrain, the physicality of the elements which in the open are like a promise of exploration, of an unfamiliar or postponed knowledge of the darkest regions of memory?

The Marvelous Concrete Outside.

In its corners, streets, gates, bars, squares, boulevards, gardens, parks and cafés, the city, as is known, maintains some of the focal points of "its" unconscious. These are found and explored everyday by surrealists who obtain the essential experience of surreality in metropolitan life. The concrete experience of exteriority (nature) and the feeling of exteriority (the city) requires from us a disposition closely akin not only to the sensible renewal of people (since the greatest promise resides herein), but also to existence and its poetic reserves, and to the revitalization of the interior life that is suffering a process of sterilization because of the convulsive technologization of interiority and the progressive forgetting of life *outside*.

The abandonment to exteriority is not an escape (nor an Edenic return), but the impulse of life toward the reconquest of itself, and in the intellectual sphere is one of the most urgent impulses at the beginning of this century. This abandonment is in no way equivalent to the Romantic sublimation of the absolute (nor do we intend to compare them within the framework of this essay). Perhaps the abandonment to exteriority engenders a somewhat more modest disposition (at least in its first formulation), despite the great depth, as if it were the restoration of the relationship with exteriority through what we might call a lesson from childhood: the discovery within the concrete of the animacy of everything, of *that* which palpitates and which we could associate with an exteriorial unconscious. This exists, it seems to me, as a *mouth of shadow* that spans its surroundings and is recognized in its objects, elements, beings, animals, plants and even humans. It's a tremulous indeterminacy, sometimes shimmering, at others vibratory, which touches, by means of forms, the key that opens all the senses, and about which there is no conscious awareness; it's something like a reverberation, born of matter itself, which encloses exteriority, with which it is integrated, like an invisible but intuited shadow and which comes from outside, not from within. I'm not by any means limiting my understanding to a mere "exterior reality," and even less should it be mistaken for some "unearthly" reality. With the mouth of shadow and its mysterious resonance, I mean to evoke the idea that it haloes the outside's depth, which should be seen as a kind of dialectic leap destined to re-enchant an interiority particularly maltreated in our epoch. The point is, finally, as a specific proposition, to see in the open the eloquence of its enigmatic tremor and derive a metaphoric energy from it (1).

Breton's words are significant in this regard, not only because his eloquent poetic analogies correspond with what inspired them (the experience of language should always aspire to be at the level of the experience of exteriority), but also because of the way it revealed his condition of infatuation, elucidating it. Here is the "the delirium of absolute presence." Life, as a drama of love, guided his wonder until he saw, fully outside, the pristine novelty within the marvels of the real, in the physicality of nature in which the feelings of his *amour fou* were prefigured.

This visionary quality of Breton, besides reaching its maximum poetic expression in certain passages of *Mad Love*, *Arcane 17* and, in another way, in the text entitled *Language in the Stones* (A. Breton, Everyday Magic, p. 137, Ed. Fundamentos, Madrid, 1975), is explicitly revealed in the choice of elements represented by some of his phrases, that is, the choice of certain natural elements that underscore the unknown morphology of the concrete marvelous of nature, to wit: the date tree, the black sand, the *sempervivum*, the white-secreting plant. Here the eye touches on the most hidden corners of the imaginary, located in plain view and full daylight. Therefore we shouldn't forget that above all he *has seen*, and that it's this vision which, through sympathy, will provide us with our readiness to see and share a fully real imaginary experience. Nor should we forget that Breton had already given us previous evidence of his attention to this unprecedented morphology of exteriority's concrete marvellous. I'm thinking of those aspects he chose in order to represent his idea of convulsive beauty; mineral, animal and botanical features, such as the aragonite, blue bells (*mésange bleue*), or coral (*la Grande Barrière*), not to mention, within another context, his fascination with the mandrake root.

Hence we can regard all this as a precedent for our own reflections, to the same degree that they open a parallel path within surrealism which can be explored in a keener as well as more generalized manner, without claiming that our own theory and approach agrees with Breton's concerns from his own time (nor which is necessary) (2).

Breton's focus on the phenomenology of the marvelous of "Earth's ultrasensitive regions," would reappear years later when he was writing *Arcane 17*. On that occasion, he was working under the burden of love, as well as under the burden of human suffering (World War II). However, I won't dwell on this text, which I think requires another kind of analysis. I'll just emphasize that, once again, an extreme force of nature (the Percé rock), in the confines of culture, made him see again how profound exteriority can bestow its gifts on the besieged and shattered human spirit, reviving his distraught interior. And it would provide him with various reflections, whose scope perhaps we haven't yet managed to comprehend.

Moreover, in 1957, *Language in the Stones* appeared in *Le Surrealisme, même*, nº3, a text that truly anticipated the experience of surreality in the outdoors. At the time Breton was living in Saint Cirq La Popie, in a setting that was no longer urban, such that the sensorial experience would change his perceptual habits and, of equal importance, his relational ones. His walks along the bed of the Lot River led him to discover certain sensorial objects that, like the stones, provided him with an unexpected knowledge of the universe, both physical and mental. He refers to this in various ways. For example, when he says "...thanks to them you can immerse yourself deeper and deeper in the image, almost empty of meaning, which most people form of the world...we're entering into the sphere of signs and signals" (op. cit. p. 138). I won't examine this in depth here, except to insist, for now, on recognizing its power as exterior surreality, which is, moreover, what occured to Breton himself, and which subsequently led him to enter this domain of signs and symbols, and which occurred, to emphasize the point, as a result of once again experiencing the energy of the absolute presence of nature's splendor. And yet, before realizing the elucidation contained in the text, he insists on sensation as the principle of illumination, even as the principle of empathy with that mineral revelation, after which "various agates of a startling beauty leapt to view…that sustained me for a long moment in the illusion that I was wandering through an earthly paradise" (op. cit. p. 141).

I myself have been awestruck before the successive appearance of fossil rocks on Greek Beach near the town of Colunga, in Asturias. As I advanced along the stony shore located at one end of the beach, I was amazed at what the ground offered to my eyes, which I contemplated, gathered and possessed, seduced by its marvelous morphology. What momentarily appeared to me as objects whose power of seduction led me to fall into a kind of perplexity caused by the patterns, striations and other forms that transformed my perception, as a result of the very place where I found them, they have settled in my memory over time, making me experience another sensation, since these stones, with their peculiarities and singularities, have all but deposited the energy of their primordial life into my own daily routine, to the degree that their presence in my domestic space is impregnated with their telluric radiations, by their magic power, concentrated in each and every spot that possesses a portion of the genius of the place where they were originally found (3).

The Unconscious of Exteriority

I'm not sure I can clearly and exactly define what I mean by the *unconscious of exteriority*, but I intuit that it becomes apparent in certain places, at certain times and in whatever it is that constitutes these places (mainly in nature, but also in certain areas of the city). In my case, these places produce a feeling of isolation, of distance, and of *suspension*. This feeling becomes acute at midday ('my' midday, which goes from 2:45 to 4:30, peaking at 3 or 3:30). Under its general atmosphere (solar, temporal, spatial), and connected with time, with places affirming the unexpected potential of their location: it's not an interior (psychic) specter that arises and guides my affectivity, but rather the specter of things: a rock, a wall, a door, a fragment of the ground, a pier, a bough, a bit of plastic, a piece of paper at rest or swept up, a root emerging from the sand, a stone, a handrail, a statue, a completely empty resort town, a road, a coastal marker, etc., undergo a transformation which lends them their ghostly, spectral aspect, made even greater by their connection with the surroundings: beneath a tense, semi-hallucinatory or hallucinatory gaze (which becomes especially acute when sunlight coincides with a clear sky but is crossed by large or enormous white clouds and a strong wind), under the influence of midday, what awakes from its indolence before my eyes (and my eyes from their own indolence) is what was just *there*: the specter of absolute presence.

Regardless of my lack of clarity concerning what I call the unconscious of exteriority, maybe this will be settled, at least in part, after the following considerations. If, as I say, I have sensed that it undulates in a specific place in the open (in the city limits and further away from them), sometimes for me it ends up taking a concrete shape in certain human constructions through which the human unconscious meets it. These structures generally tend to establish a limit. For example a mile-long handrail along some sea cliffs in an enclave at the limit of an abandoned village, or a border stone, whether it's on the coast, a plateau or in the mountains, or a country road or the remains of one, or a bridge, or a dam, including the absurd and ridiculous signpost in the shape of pole and street sign which in reality is a road situated between the coast and a mountain.

On the one hand, it happens that time, bad weather or erosion give these structures a certain *loss* of function that ends up becoming their ally, as if all this wear has forced them to mimic the surroundings and convert them into an additional element, an osmotic element between the artificial and the natural, although acquiring their own presence, as if they were becoming charged with *anima.*

Then on the other hand, there is the circumstance where these structures manifest a foreign quality in the place where they arise, provoking a sensation of strangeness that stimulates the oneiric imagination, so it is not too unbelievable to contemplate the setting in which these structures are situated as a fragment from a daydream.

But there are other aspects which, supplementing the ones already mentioned, distinguish themselves by having a significant meaning and which ultimately would bring more concreteness to the notion of the unconscious of exteriority.

I have in mind here the border stones and their function as demarcators of the terrain; these stones that flank the roads in the rural areas. It is important to take note the experience that they provoke and its twofold nature. For a start, there is no doubt that their function as topographic mediators brings a certain subliminal prohibition against passing them, as if they worked as indicators to reveal that what lies beyond them is the unknown, danger, and all that *frightens*. Whoever has lived or spent the majority of one's childhood in a village, and who passes through its back roads and side roads, would possibly feel this sensation more than once: the sensation of being prevented from going any further, as it would mean a distressing separation from the village, from the security that the village gives. Then here is also the similar experience with these same roads, dirt roads whose curves are indicators of what is beyond them, of how far they can lead or of what is hidden behind them. In other words, to go further than the outskirts ("at the village exit" as they used to say), to pass the limit imposed by the border stone or the curves of the road that warn us not to come into contact – this being said with very poetic and eloquent words – with "the ghosts who come to meet us" as Murnau, with his visionary skill had us witness in *Nosferatu*. And the fact is that if these structures exercise a psychological control over us because of the unconscious fear or anxiety that they can provoke (because danger does occur there), it is rightly through them that something drives to surpass them, to confront fear and venture into the region where *the spirits of the earth* are trembling. Who hasn't found himself in the situation of seeing a border stone with a number on it, at the edge of a dirt road, without wanting to find the next one that follows with increasing distance? Or, as I already suggested: who hasn't felt the irresistible curiosity to arrive at one curve of a road only to continue to the next, and then to proceed from curve to curve in such a successive way? Or being attracted to a house in the open countryside, in total solitude, whose mystery appeals to us as the spirit of childhood leads us to it, disregarding any instinct toward security. In fact, one could finish by saying that it is necessary to feel afraid (or at least that sensation of fear which is associated with the taste for the unknown), because this sensation forces us to reclaim our own psyche, our mental disposition towards our meeting with the disquieting-marvelous, to the extent that this fear is a manifestation of the marvelous in its hidden flow which is latent in full exteriority.

I recognize within my appetite and fascination for these human structures, to which I referred, the persistence of a childhood experience that I suspect moreover is more common than anything else. I acknowledge within them the elements that invite me to take the direction towards the unknown that pulses with full exteriority, with all its anxiety but also with all its promise of the marvelous. This double feeling is complementary, one could say, and acquired its most memorable expression within me one day when, as a kid, while crossing a bridge that stretched across a stream at the village exit and which was reached by a road that bordered a threshing floor (from which the abundant rain had washed the dirt from its side walls one morning, uncovering many human skeletons, which made a strong impression on me, as it appeared that the old cemetery of the village had been located beneath it), I met a stranger who, without any reason, provoked only by my imagination and the weight of rural legend, I identified as *the man with the sack.* This terrible figure, at least according to what our parents used to tell us, kidnapped the children and put them in a sack (which provoked a panic terror in us), embodies for me, forever after, the human face of the unconscious of exteriority: the simultaneously terrifying and irresistible expression of *the ghost who comes to meet us* (here I return to the phrase from *Nosferatu*, of which I reproduce in its entirety: "And as he crossed the bridge, the ghosts came to meet him"), at once attractive and luminous, with human form, and whom one could never leave for another, as if receding further and further from childhood led adult life to its "happy loss," or its yearning to go astray and recover its capacity to establish a relationship with the unreasonable, the unintelligible, the monstrous and thus, the captivating. (4)

Looking From the Outside...

I wonder, furthermore, what would be the best way to bear visual witness to this absolute presence, and to indicate its potential for surreality. What landscape or landscapes, besides those elements already mentioned, and which display such a tangible aspect, would embody this absolute presence and could indicate – each one according to its *fall* into them – their mouth of shadow? Everything leads me to believe that the photographic document becomes a revelatory agent of the first order. Not so much because it represents or responds to my question, but rather that through it a visual precision can be attained in accordance with the gaze that guides it, always obeying it. The photographic document appears to me as evidence of the correlation between the objective and subjective, which it enlists to participate in its singular strangeness, since it exceeds the external aspect of exteriority (its apparent appearance) and leads, as I mentioned before, to an apprehension of the profundity of exteriority. Because the landscape is also a latency, and with the exception that its orographic constitution reveals it to be a patently oneiric space (which leads toward the evident), most landscapes contain a surreality potential (where the evident has been excluded and remains as a latency). The apprehension of this potential for surreality will depend entirely on the perceptual state of the observer: that is, on a blindness to what precedes this perception (culturalizing factors) and its innocence before what is unknown to it (what opens as a limit). In fact, before any new landscape, whatever we know disappears and becomes suspended in memory in accordance with how this new territory appreciably impregnates our perception and emotions (5). What I'm saying, you might think, is patently obvious, but that doesn't invalidate the waking dream it produces, with all its distinctive intensity.

Nonetheless, I want to emphasize that in approaching perception in this way, I do it while keeping in mind that the act of perceiving is a way of relating to exteriority (of being outside and of seeing from the outside). I remember being in this mindset on the 2nd of January, 2006, and I see myself with a lost look – not introverted, however, but extroverted. The situation was this: I was sitting in a chair on the banks of the Tajo River, not far from where it empties into the Atlantic. Nearby there was a structure that looked both like a lighthouse and a chimney. I fixed my gaze on it, but it also wandered to the other side of the river, toward the faces of some friends who had accompanied me, but above all, it rested on the far-reaching and very white glare off the water produced by a limpid sun. This glare, I realized sometime later, was both the origin

and the objective of my gaze. That is, my gaze found its limit there, and it revealed an awareness of its extroversion.

A chance event would make this awareness even sharper (at that moment, less than its persistence would make on me later on). There was a moment when I interrupted this state of contemplation and got up from my chair. I looked here and there distractedly and also at the chair. To my great astonishment I discovered, written on the seat, the word MIRAR (look). This occurrence seemed doubly extraordinary to me. On the one hand it crystallized my state of contemplation (my distant look). On the other, the word was written in Spanish (this occurred in Lisbon, and in Portuguese the word look is *olhar*.)

When seriously considering the factors that made up this episode – the date (January 2nd), the place (Lisbon, a city at the western extreme), the spot (the banks of a river delta), the word written in Spanish in another country and its exact coincidence with my action (looking) – I can't help but think that everything culminated in the confirmation that the act of looking is the same as being outside, a foreignness, and that, with at least the same significance that one experiences intense and singular interior visions, exteriority also provides visions characterized by a powerful and singular intensity.

If looking is to be outside, and a foreignness, then its result, which is seeing, suggests that we're always in a borderline situation, at the edge…

Awareness of the Form and Visualization of Surreality in the Open

I distinguish three circumstances in which visual form acquired through the experience of surreality within exteriority becomes tangible (giving priority here to nature). They are something like three realms of vision that combine, while still preserving their complete independence: the conceptual, the imaginary, and the manifest. I'm speaking here always in terms of concrete realms.

Conceptual: An idea contains a latent morphology for which an external form must be sought.

For example: Mirage is a word that clearly (the irony is intentional) indicates a state of perceptual perturbation proportional to the mental one according to which the appearance of the real is involuntarily subjected to judgment, or at least remains in an absolute state of suspension. However, it's not exactly the mirage as a phenomenon that I want to elucidate, but another state that nevertheless might belong to the same genealogy. I'm referring to fainting, falling unconscious (which I use metaphorically, of course). In alluding to this condition, subsequently I'll do the same for what follows, that is, the restoration of consciousness. What I mean is that after losing consciousness, and the restoration that follows, or more precisely, the interval that occurs between the two states (just before returning to complete lucidity) is when the relationship to things becomes reestablished. But while appearing to be like themselves, these objects are no longer equivalent to themselves, and that what one sees, is perceived with such a weight of ambiguity, of indeterminacy, and displays such a degree of transformation, that the thing in itself experiences a liberation from the principle of identity and suffers a severe shock that leaves it exposed to its own polysemous aspect. Basically I mean to suggest that it's not absolutely necessary to know or to have knowledge (in the sense of being erudite, of being encyclopedic, of being 'cultured') in order to have a poetic experience of the real (surreality) and that this is fully revealed by virtue of its unpredictable and immeasurable affectivity.

The selection of photographs presented are testimony to this mental state and its encounter with the real *at the poetic edge of appearance*, or viewed from the opposite perspective, when the poetic encounters the real through that which suddenly appears.

Imaginary: Nature offers more possibilities for encounter than for pursuit: one comes to nature without seeking, and it commences with an encounter, though one discovers oneself less by extension than by penetration. This elemental truth is one of the highest forms of relation with nature, and I'm inclined to think that through it we can begin to unravel part of our own mystery, in the very fabric of correspondences. It's a question of vertigo, because turning our gaze towards nature effectively means returning to a less docile perception ("the eye in an untamed state" Breton called it), allowing us to feel its effect on us in a more revelatory way. A gaze that expands the coordinates of the relationship between

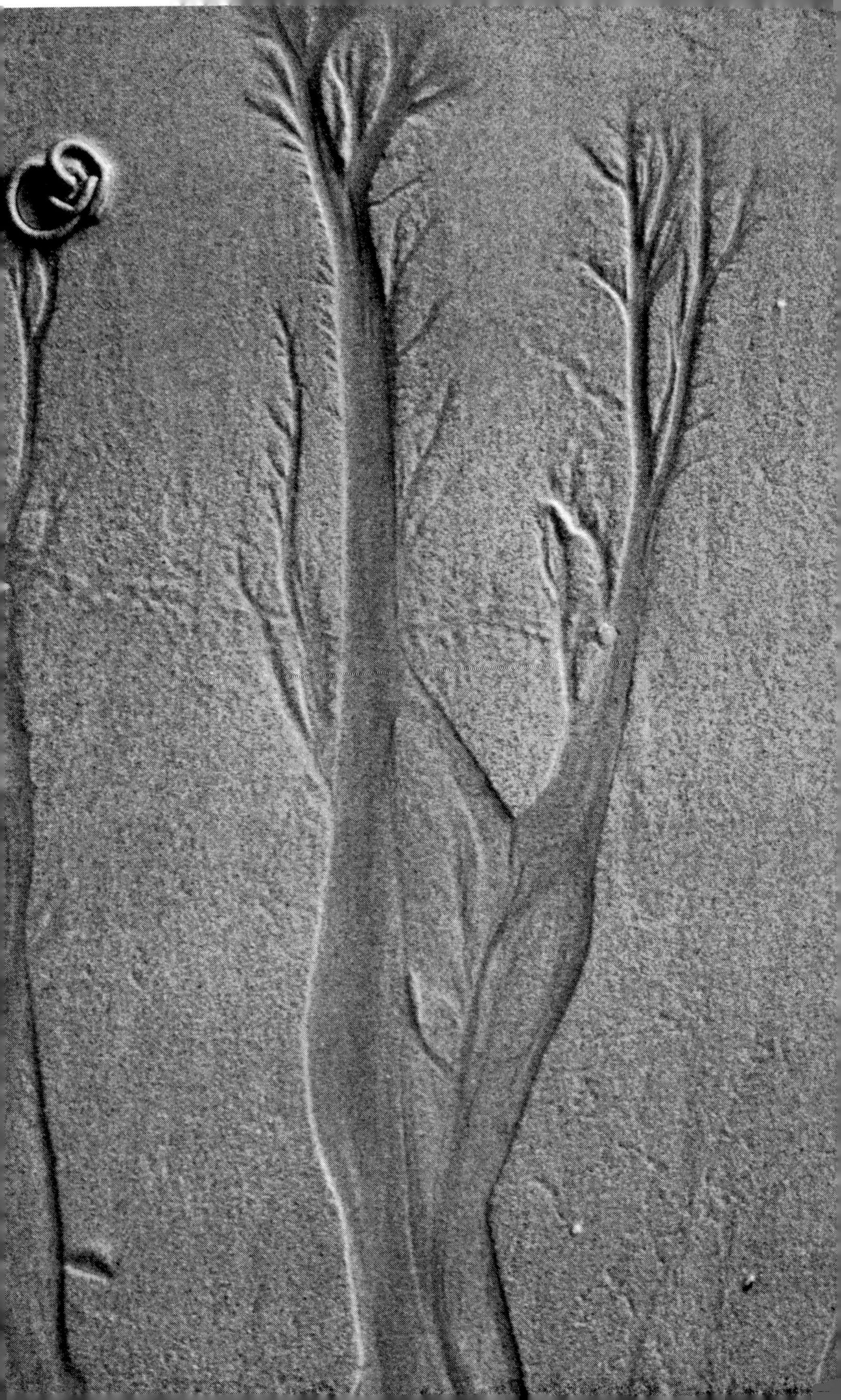

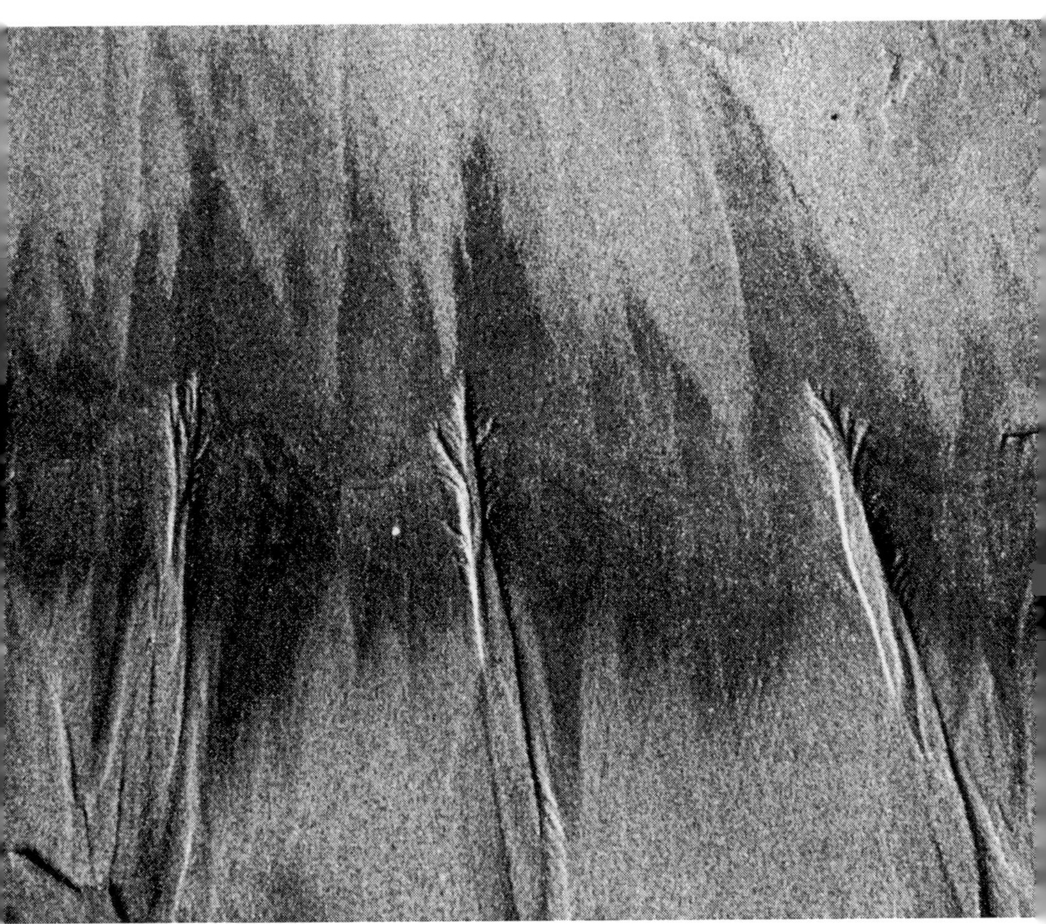

external and internal life, taking its dialogue as far as possible. In the particular context of a poetic relationship with nature, an analogical approach is among the most apt for its clarification and advancement. We shouldn't forget that most cosmogonies of the first human societies make use of the analogical 'tool' as a mode of knowledge and of relation to the 'world,' nor that analogical knowledge, with the appearance of so-called Modernity, has been progressively replaced by what is too complacently designated as logic.

It's now the task of poets to oppose this latest deductive method with a new form of correspondence that would guide us to a reencounter with our absent reality. Poetic analogy unravels the knot and follows the thread that leads to the consummation of the encounter. There's no doubt that surrealism in our time has opened a breach in the wall through which poetic analogy can enter. In the broad spectrum of surrealism's relational procedures, poetic analogy has restored and revitalized the entire field of relations between perception and representation with extraordinary vigor. Among them, and now more forcefully than in the past, photography, without doubt, is a medium which I'm inclined to see as an instrument for revealing the *poetic materialism* of the sensible world, and through which new routes can be opened in the domain of the visionary. In this sense, photography, specifically in this context, has been asked to serve as an "interior model," configuring a world whose reality renders pallid, in what it contains of the illusory, that other reality of immediate data that we must endure. Because reality, given its uniqueness, persists in casting glances meant to attract our static attention, glances whose line of sight evokes in its anticipation the existence of unforeseen ghosts. Accordingly, by means of photography it's possible to capture certain visual accidents that question the fixed dimensions of external reality. It brings to light a subterranean world of forms, lost in the drudgery of routine, which in revealing them tends to objectify an absent reality. A significant correspondence is produced, in this regard, between photography's vision and an interior one in their relations with natural space. This is made more explicit when the natural realm is explored *macroscopically* (and here my previous remarks become clearer). This macroscopic vision, which in the analogical sphere represents an interior look, allows the eye to exercise an extremely profound scrutiny of nature. In itself constituting a highly relevant visionary operation, this macro-photographic view tends to reveal nature's own visionary dimension, and about which it can be claimed, at the very least, that it's composed of both the exquisite stuff of exaltation and the visually tempting substance of the voluptuous.

Such a vision builds a bridge in which poetic and natural revelations coincide. It's this kind of vision that animates the encounter of these revelations through their latent affinities, that is, through the immanent correspondence to (its) analogical life. Hence, a unifying principle is produced, entirely on the surface, as a result, and which overcomes the total preeminence of one thing over another. In fact, beyond all preeminence, the fluid circulation of both revelations is encouraged by the life that illuminates them.

Under the dictates of this primordial and unpredictable encounter, photographs of tree trunks by Javier Gálvez *(The Forest of Signs)*, and of forms in the sand by Eugenio Castro, both present themselves as shimmering reflections through which we apprehend that novel morphology of the concrete marvelous that covers the surface and displays itself in its absolute presence.

Manifest: The photographic fragment of an affective space is one of the best ways to convey its atmosphere, which communicates with its surreality potential. This fragment maintains a relationship, according to what is being observed, with a macro-photographic vision, or with that of a close-up with wide depth-of-field, proportional to the size of the object (a place, the elements of a place) that in its highest optical concreteness tends to extract a fascination for the concrete. This is how this appreciation for the concrete ends by accentuating its *estranging* quality. In this photographic 'centering,' which is the technical result of a *vision that precedes it*, the places and sites (we could add, its objects and its faces, its forms and objects), appear equally estranged. The photographic fragment favors the scene that best represents this latency that I associate with an unconscious of exteriority. This fragment is the *viewpoint* with the most visual precision (which induces an awareness of the uniqueness of forms), since through it both the mental image and poetic operation meet and share, in objectifying, with a subjective vision, the ghost of the open: the absolute presence of concrete forms.

1. On this point I can't insist enough on Dalí's representations of the metamorphosis, that lead to some of the culminating moments of his most visionary years. It's important to emphasize the convergence that Dalí establishes between exteriority and the unconscious, due to the persistence in his memory of a place that determined everything he would accomplish in his lifetime. This place, which led to his universal triumph, is the genesis of his ideas regarding the ghost and the specter so masterfully developed in his text *The New Colors Of Spectral Sex Appeal.* But if we wish to see them displayed in all their splendor and – to use a term so significant for Dalí – perturbation, we should conscientiously examine, time and again, the clouds, rocks, beaches and the symbiosis which he establishes between the light and shadow of the landscape of Cabo de Creus in all its depth and amplitude. This place, as is well known, was for Dalí one of the tangible phenomena of nature that nurtured his extraordinary and delirious capacity for association and simulation. His theory of concrete irrationality, developed so masterfully by the painter and which contributed so significantly to consolidating his notion of the surreality, can be found there unambiguously.

2. A notable attempt to develop this notion was made by the Paris Group of the Surrealist Movement. In 1993, issue number 3 of the magazine *S.U.RR...* was inspired by *Géographie passionnelle.* Broader than the project undertaken here, and for that reason less specific, that's where the differences between the approaches of one and another reside, though there exits a further, more important one: the point isn't, in my opinion, to go forth to an encounter with what an interior solicitude confirms, but rather to be outside and from *there* restore to interiority its lost, hibernating or colonized powers. This is not antagonistic, because it's not founded on a separating dualism, though it does express dispositions that highlight singularities. In fact, you could say that there exists a point that coincides to a large degree with the viewpoint of my French colleagues: when "it's discovered just how the exaltation of the imagination is connected to the spirit of place...and the latent meaning of the metamorphoses which the place gives rise to are apprehended" (Guy Girard, *Vers une géographie passionelle.* Op. cit. pg. 6, Paris, 1993). In any case, both dispositions must be understood as complementary.

3. The fascination exercised by rocks and stones on the surrealists is significant. Limiting myself to the present, I agree with Guy Girard when, in his account of the cliffs of Flammanville, and in particular his description of certain of its rock formations, he suggests that, like *Le dent de Saturne* and *Pierre au Rey*, they produce dreams. Girard recounts the following: "One night in the autumn of 1980, walking near the lighthouse, I noticed that, in the field next to me, one of the big rocks, similar to a heavyset *menhir,* had been turned upside down, revealing beneath it an enormous hole, perhaps the entrance to a subterranean passage or maybe a funerary chamber. I entered and found myself in front of a skeleton that seemed to guard a treasure from the time of the Gauls. Invaded by fear, I run away through a passageway that, as I moved down it, became a gallery of Parisian catacombs where I encounter Breton and Aragon, dressed as they would have been in the 1920s" (Guy Girard, *Baligan,* in the magazine *S.U.RR...* nº 3, pg. 28, devoted to the above cited *Géographie passionelle*). The stroll around the area surrounding the cliff leads the poet, via his dream, to realize that previously other spirits similar to him (that is, other surrealists, friends or not, whose visit to the same area he was ignorant of) had wandered around this place and, as was the case of Claude Tarnaud, had remarked on its "initiatic character" (Guy Girard, Op. cit. p. 29).

This last consideration is not so unusual, given that confronted by these massive rock faces whose power evokes a sentient life oriented toward an encounter with whatever in it had been able to remain in a cloistered state, some of us are restored to ourselves, though by way of a feeling of remoteness, a way of relating that approaches animism. And if it's true that the celebration of this encounter usually occurs on an individual plane, we shouldn't forget that the stimulus that this particular celebration generates supposes sowing, for a single being, the seeds of a future, perhaps less solitary celebration. The point here is to relearn, recuperate ancestral memory and reactivate, with our own ceremonies, however modest, those which, like the Australian aborigines "are destined to extract…the spiritual power that impregnates the great rocks" (John Michell, *L'Esprit de la terre ou le génie du lieu*, p. 62, Seuil) In fact, there's a lesson to be learned from this, since, as with the aborigines (or the oracles, who extract their visions from the resonant stones), the itinerary of the vision becomes inverted, from the moment when one begins to see *through a stone's eyes*; that is to say, the gaze, in its outside—*which becomes aware of form*—is what injects its incantatory potential into the spirit.

This happens when a natural phenomenon reveals itself before our eyes to such an exceptional degree that it stimulates the feeling of physical dreaming and excites our visionary capacity. As I write this, I'm reminded of the stones that provoked visions in Silvia Guiard in a popular ritual (the link with animism is here explicit, and we feel empathy with this anthropological episode), which she shares with us in her book *Quebrada* (Tsé=Tsé, Buenos Aires, Argentina, 1998) The poets declares there: "They select them, they gather them up, they bring them over. Preferably white ones. With love, with respect, they pile them up: stones and more stones are stacked in layers, towards the sky they climb, they hurry upward, they form a mountain in miniature, sweet nipple that sprouts from the Earth which spins… swirling towards the sky—but also a deep well of silence, opening to the double depths of life's fall towards the shadowy tunnels."

"With love, with respect, they pile them up: each one their stone. Are they stones or bones? Aren't they perhaps their very bodies, stacked up one on top of the other…that forms the sacred mountain?

Each one their stone. Each one their portion of life-death, their mark on time. Each one their kidney of laughter and kidney of tears. The community creates its navel and dances lovingly around it." (Op. cit. pg. 39)

"What do I have, stone, in my hands? What do I myself put on the pile? What do I have, stone, light, shadow-play, knot, in my hands?"…"Here, where one dreams. Where one gently works, dreaming the presences and forms. Who's coming? Who walks there? Who whispers?" (Op. cit. pg. 40)

"The stone beats. It Dreams.

Adorned, the mound anxiously awaits the mysterious nativity that on Saturday will again take place among its stones: its opening, its shine, its apogee. The burst of its light." (Op. cit. pg. 41)

The imagination of nature and the imagination of man meet. Our eyes don't merge with the rocks, they see with the rocks' eyes, with the stones' eyes. In short: they see. I experienced something like this when I wrote *Love Letter to a Mountain* that at the time I called *On El Torcal Mountain, Sesame Multiplied.* I revisited the episode in which this entire mass of rocks opens to me the vision of *Castle in the Pyrenees*, after the painting by René Magritte: "In truth, the entire idea that I was able to form of what was hidden beyond the door of that castle, of how and of what its various floors, galleries and rooms were constructed, and how they were laid out, I comprehended now on this mountain: it's the *interior* which appears in this landscape and which forces us to rub our eyes with the back of our hands over and over again…And behind its entryway, built from the breath of the elements, open a thousand more so that wishing to lose himself he will hear in the mineral verb the whisper that notifies him of his lost likeness. It's the delirium of nature, absolutely! Nature, which opens to poetic thinking an unprecedented realm to explore. And this thinking recognizes itself in these places that she has created for stupefaction."

Furthermore, I earlier referred to "ancestral memory" and to "reactivating with our own ceremonies…," to which I would add: to find the images that embody it in our present. I'll return to this question later. Now I'd like to mention a photographic document provided by Bruno Jacobs in 2006. It's a series of illustrations depicting eleven rocks on whose surface a series of inscriptions and words characteristic of the signatures of graffiti artists have been carved. Jacobs, who had completely forgotten the text by Breton referred to above, called his document *The Language of Rocks*. What's remarkable about all this is the wonderful concatenation of 'differed' meanings and coincidences produced. On one hand, Jacobs' unconscious expresses itself with complete affinity for a text that had disappeared from his consciousness; an affinity for its form and for its orientation. On the other, the encounter with these rocks and the language inscribed in them, causes the return of the repressed to the present time, which acquires a new form and a new formulation which, and the association is crucial, activates ancestral memory. Moreover, as an involuntary ally of it all, another equally crucial association can't be ignored: the graffiti on the rocks newly proclaims, to give just one example, the petroglyphs of antiquity, in such a way that an apparently dead language is rehabilitated by means of a modern poetic procedure (always in Rimbaud's sense), that hasn't lost its ancestral memory; a language that hasn't become separated from its initial murmurings in which a unique and latent meaning is contained.

(4) Isn't that what happens to Ana, the girl from *The Spirit of the Beehive*, that movie of Víctor Erice, when she crosses the railroad tracks (clear border with the village – reason and logic – and passage to the land of the spirits – the unconscious of exteriority) and goes towards that isolated house in the middle of the plain that powerfully calls upon her attention to meet the first "man with a sack," the fugitive who hides in it? (We never really get to know whether it is a "delinquent" or a guerrilla rebel, but everything denotes him as a social and political monster who ultimately has to be dispatched, as it so happens.) Doesn't Ana constantly return to the well to look at the bottom, at the water (the depth of exteriority) in order to see if that other monster, Frankenstein's monster, will surface? After having been led by her father to the solitary and isolated house, and after Ana discovers him, leaves running and takes flight without feeling fear, and spending the night away from the refuge and familial protection – doesn't she meet the monster on the bank of the stream on whose waters she sees her face being mirrored, and further still, sees him approaching her from behind? It wouldn't be arbitrary or exaggerated to recognize Frankenstein's monster in *the man with the sack*. Maybe one should remember that "the monster" Frankenstein is earning his life, as he needs to have the childhood that never was nor had been given him: he is born as a man without his own life behind him, but instead with a predetermined existence subject to the scientific imperative of creating a social monster with the collective unconscious (the "monster," let us not forget, is made of "remnants" of various human types). Frankenstein is consequently born already perverse, as maturely (adultly) perverse – however paradoxical it may seem – thus deprived of the child's "polymorphic perversion." However, in light of such a fact, I ask myself the following: how can he not want to possess the spirit of the girl who offers him the flowers, and to acknowledge in her what is lacking within his own being: a

childhood life that would grant him a humanity that wasn't monsterly. Through his perverse actions, Frankenstein revolts against scientific determinism and grants himself what had been mutilated within him; the polymorphic perverse that restores his humanity and leads him to overcome this monstrous hybridization. In fact, something happens in the movie we are commenting on which inverts the dark legend of our sinister figure: Ana who wants to meet the monster and to relate to it, rebels against that dark legend, and instead of hiding or being afraid of getting lost, abandons herself to the encounter, filled with apprehension and perplexity. The depth of exteriority and that of the human mind coincide here and surpass their duality. Childhood life projects onto adult life unheard-of promises that are to be fulfilled.

5. But something else also occurs, which is not the opposite: we return to the places we've experienced, which are usually those that are unchanging and at the same time perpetually renewed. Consider, for example, revisiting the same ocean, the same city, the same mountain, whose mere recollection makes up the very respiration of the new experience. And the following frequently occurs as well: an encounter with the new in the already experienced but still unknown. An experience of the other embodied in the totality; a singularization of the commonplace. Since ultimately, what are rocks, soil, mountains? Common places suddenly renewed by a gaze that, *through them*, is itself renewed.

Biographical Data

Mattias Forshage (Stockholm, 1968). Surrealist poet and biologist in Stockholm, Sweden. He has been active for a very long time in the Surrealist Group of Stockholm as a theorist, organiser, game player and wanderer, and does his professional work in entomology systematics.

Miguel Pérez Corrales (Las Palmas, Canarias, 1955). Completely identified with the surrealist revolution since the discovery of the Manifestoes at the age of sixteen. Has published the following surrealist books: *Lorelei del sur*, *El ojo del perenquén*, *La conjura de Ulises*, *Nagom Kême*, *Mares y fábulas*, *Tribus remotas*, *La flor del Ancón*, *Cité Toyen*, *La estalagmita*, *La isla invisible*, *Disparos del archibrazo* (photography) and *Póker de fuegos*. An enthusiast of Blues, Hot Jazz, old Portugal (its nature and people) and Canarian cock fighting, of which he is chronicler and historian.

José Manuel Rojo (Madrid, 1964). Has been a part of the Surrealist Group of Madrid since 1987. He has collaborated in all of the collective publications of the group, especially in the journal Salamandra, as well as in certain editions of the Pepitas de Calabaza imprint (*Alfred Jarry and Pataphysics, Enrico Baj, Laurent Tailhade*). Has devoted his existence to social liquidation and the triumph of true life, but doesn't know if he will witness the great day of the attack on the sky, and, in that case, whether he will live up to the circumstances. Although this doubt bothers him, he finds strength in the thought that people also consider him a fanatic.

Bruno Jacobs (Brussels, Belgium 1952). Initiator of the Surrealist Group of Stockholm in 1985 in which he was active until 2000. Collaborator to *Salamandra*, journal of the Surrealist Group of Madrid. Friend of the clouds, poet of temperate disposition and a visceral internationalist.

Guy Girard (La Hague, France 1959). Painter and poet, and discovered surrealism in 1977. Has lived in Paris since 1984 and participated in the collective activity of the "Paris group of the surrealist movement" from 1990 to 2007. Recently he has been part of the international exhibition of Surrealism today, *The Reverse of the Look* in Coimbra, Portugal. He has specially published a collection of essays *L'ombre et la demande. Projections surréalistes* by the Atelier de Création Libertaire (2005) and a book of poetry *L'oreiller du souffleur* (2008). He is also a translator of Portuguese surrealist poetry, and wonders about the analogies between surrealism and certain aspects of Taoism.

Manuel Crespo (Barcelona, 1963). Has been in contact with the Surrealist Group of Madrid since 1998. He has published the poetry book *Guía de perplejos* (1998) and collective publications *Indicios de Salamandra*, *Los días en rojo* and *Situación de la poesía (por otros medios) a la luz del surrealismo*. His greatest interest is in the life of a poetic-social upheaval.

Eric W. Bragg (New Orleans, 1971). Now lives in the Berkeley/San Francisco area. He is a dreamer, an explorer, a poet who uses material, plastic forms of expression, and a warrior who fights boredom. His work can be found at *www.surrealcoconut.com.*

Ángel Zapata (Madrid, 1961). Published *La práctica del relato* (1997), *Las buenas intenciones y otros cuentos* (2001), *El vacío y el centro: Tres lecturas en torno al cuento breve* (2002), and *La vida ausente* (2007), as well as the translations of Michel Carrouges' *André Breton y los datos fundamentales del surrealismo* (2008) and Louis Janover's *Poesía y revolución* (2007). He is a member of the Surrealist Group of Madrid.

Noé Ortega Quijano (Madrid, 1984). Has practically lived for his whole life in Santander. A member of the Surrealist Group of Madrid, contributing to their various publications and collective projects with texts concerning the urban subconscious, tactilism, and the detournement of public advertisements, just to name a few.

Julio Monteverde (Cartagena, 1973). A member of the Surrealist Group of Madrid since 2001. He has published the book of poems *La luz de los días* (2002), and the chapbook *Planetario* (2007). Has written introductions for editions of *Apollinaire* and *Oskar Panizza* for the imprint Pepitas de Calabaza, and has collaborated on various periodicals, especially for the journal *Salamandra*.

Vicente Gutiérrez-Escudero (Santander, 1977). A member of the Surrealist Group of Madrid. He has published the book of poems *Mimo muerto* (2001). His essays can be found in collective publications such as *Situación de la poesía (por otros medios) a la luz del surrealismo* and in the Madrid group's journal *Salamandra*. He practices visual and experimental poetry, oneirism, mathematics and eroticism. He loves everyday surprises.

Silvia Guiard (Buenos Aires, 1957). A member of the Signo Ascendente Group and its continuation, the Surrealist Group of Buenos Aires, which was active collectively until 1992. Her article *Buenos Aires: el surrealismo en la lucha contra la dictadura* outlines the history of the spoken experience.

She has published various books of poetry: *Salomé o la búsqueda del cuerpo*, *Los banquetes errantes: diario de viajes*, *Quebrada*, *En el reino blanco*, and the chapbooks *Mujer-pájaro en el círculo del sol* y *Lombrices* (for children).

Eugenio Castro (Toledo-las Herencias, 1959). Cofounder of the Surrealist Group of Madrid and their journal, *Salamandra: Surrealist intervention. Insurgent imagination. Critique of daily life.* He has published the following books: *H* and *Mal de confín* and the chapbooks: *La ciudad constelada*, *La región insomne* and *La Maga de la Masturbación.*

Street wanderer suffering from the inertia of looking. He often falls into inaction. An abolitionist of work and disdainful of effort and an epic of uselessness. His libido is augmented by the presence of certain objects, and others that he constructs. He loves the ocean.

Appendix: about the texts

- *Worthless Places,* Mattias Forshage, was published in a shorter version, also announcing a collective book on the subject that was however never realized, in *Stora Saltet,* #7, June 1997, the journal of the Surrealist group in Stockholm. Photos by Bruno Jacobs. Translated by Mattias Forshage.

- *Ceramics, Tuna Fisheries and Copper Mines,* Miguel P. Corrales, published in *Salamandra. Comunicación surrealista. Imaginación insurgente. Crítica de la vida cotidiana,* # 8/9, 1997-98, journal of the Surrealist Group in Madrid. Photos by Miguel P. Corrales. Translated by Eric W. Bragg and Bruno Jacobs.

- *The Sound of Chains: The Gothic Sentiment within Industrial Archaeology,* José Manuel Rojo, published in *Salamandra. Comunicación surrealista. Imaginación insurgente. Crítica de la vida cotidiana,* # 10, 1999. Photos by José Manuel Rojo. Translated by Eric W. Bragg.

- *The Presence of Emptiness,* Bruno Jacobs, published in *Salamandra. Intervención surrealista. Imaginación insurgente. Crítica de la vida cotidiana,* # 13-14, 2003-04, and in *El Día,* Teneriffe, 20 July 2005. Translated by Eric W. Bragg and Bruno Jacobs.

- *Poetic Spaces,* Bruno Jacobs, published in *Salamandra. Intervención surrealista. Imaginación insurgente. Crítica de la vida cotidiana,* #15/16, 2005-06. Photos by Bruno Jacobs. Translated by Eric W. Bragg and Bruno Jacobs.

- *Baligan,* Guy Girard, published in *S.U.RR...*#3, 1999, journal of the Paris group of the Surrealist Movement. Photos by Guy Girard. Translated by Eric W. Bragg and Bruno Jacobs.

- *Garraf,* Manuel Crespo, earlier version published in *Salamandra. Intervención surrealista. Imaginación insurgente. Crítica de la vida cotidiana,* # 15/16, 2005-06. Photos by Manuel Crespo. Translated by Terry Berne.

- *The Poetic Scars of Obsolescence,* Eric W. Bragg. Photos by Eric W. Bragg.

-*We Desire to Desire (Communication about a magnetic surfacing in Fuencarral street),* Ángel Zapata. Photo by Ángel Zapata. Translated by Eric W. Bragg and Bruno Jacobs.

- *The Magnetized Land,* Noé Ortega Quijano. Photos by Noé Ortega Quijano. Translated by Eric W. Bragg and Bruno Jacobs.

- *Beyond the Walls of the City,* Julio Monteverde. Translated by Eric W. Bragg and Bruno Jacobs.

The Exteriority Crisis: from the city limits and beyond

- *Three Places*, Vicente Gutiérrez. Photos by Vicente Gutiérrez. Translated by Terry Berne.

- *Finis Urbis*, José Manuel Rojo. Photos by José Manuel Rojo. Translated by Eric W. Bragg and Bruno Jacobs.

- *Eyes of Water*, Silvia Guiard. Photos by Silvia Guiard. Translated by Terry Berne.

- *Surreality and Exteriority*, Eugenio Castro. Photos by Eugenio Castro. Translated by Terry Berne, Eric W. Bragg and Bruno Jacobs.